James De Mille

The lily and the cross

A tale of Acadia

James De Mille

The lily and the cross
A tale of Acadia

ISBN/EAN: 9783741175671

Manufactured in Europe, USA, Canada, Australia, Japa

Cover: Foto ©Andreas Hilbeck / pixelio.de

Manufactured and distributed by brebook publishing software (www.brebook.com)

James De Mille

The lily and the cross

A Meeting in Mid Ocean. Page 27.

THE

LILY AND THE CROSS.

A TALE OF ACADIA.

BY

PROF. JAMES DE MILLE,

AUTHOR OF "THE DODGE CLUB," "CORD AND CREESE," "THE B. O. W. C. STORIES," "THE YOUNG DODGE CLUB," ETC.

ILLUSTRATED.

BOSTON:
LEE AND SHEPARD, PUBLISHERS.
NEW YORK:
LEE, SHEPARD AND DILLINGHAM.
1875.

Entered, according to Act of Congress, in the year 1874,
BY LEE AND SHEPARD,
In the Office of the Librarian of Congress, at Washington.

Electrotyped at the Boston Stereotype Foundry,
No. 19 Spring Lane.

CONTENTS.

CHAPTER I.
A VOICE OUT OF THE DEEP. . . . . PAGE 9

CHAPTER II.
A MEETING IN MID OCEAN. 20

CHAPTER III.
NEW FRIENDS. 31

CHAPTER IV.
MIMI AND MARGOT. 41

CHAPTER V.
A STRANGE REVELATION. 52

CHAPTER VI.
A FRENCH FRIGATE. 64

CHAPTER VII.
CAUGHT IN A TRAP. 71

CHAPTER VIII.
UNDER ARREST. 83

CHAPTER IX.
Grand Pre. 91

CHAPTER X.
Alone in the World. 103

CHAPTER XI.
A Friend in Need. 114

CHAPTER XII.
The Parson among the Philistines. 125

CHAPTER XIII.
A Stroke for Liberty. 135

CHAPTER XIV.
Manœuvres of Zac. 145

CHAPTER XV.
Flight. 154

CHAPTER XVI.
Reunion. 163

CHAPTER XVII.
Among Friends. 172

CHAPTER XVIII.
Louisbourg. 180

CHAPTER XIX.
The Captive and the Captors. 189

CHAPTER XX.
EXAMINATIONS. 198

CHAPTER XXI.
A RAY OF LIGHT. 207

CHAPTER XXII.
ESCAPE. 217

CHAPTER XXIII.
PURSUIT. 226

CHAPTER XXIV.
ZAC AND MARGOT. 235

CHAPTER XXV.
THE COURT MARTIAL. 245

CHAPTER XXVI.
NEWS FROM HOME. 255

THE LILY AND THE CROSS.

A TALE OF ACADIA.

CHAPTER I.

A VOICE OUT OF THE DEEP.

ONCE upon a time there was a schooner belonging to Boston which was registered under the somewhat singular name of the "Rev. Amos Adams." This was her formal title, used on state occasions, and was, no doubt, quite as appropriate as the more pretentious one of the "Duke of Marlborough," or the "Lord Warden." As a general thing, however, people designated her in a less formal manner, using the simpler and shorter title of the "Parson." Her owner and commander was a tall, lean, sinewy young man, whose Sunday-go-to-meeting name was Zion Awako Cox, but who was usually referred to by an ingenious combination of the initials of these three names, and thus became Zac, and occasionally Zachariah. This was the schooner which, on a fine May morning, might have been seen "bounding over the billows" on her way to the North Pole.

About her motion on the present occasion, it must

be confessed there was not much bounding, nor much billow. Nor, again, would it have been easy for any one to see her, even if he had been brought close to her; for the simple reason that the "Parson," as she went on her way, carrying Zac and his fortunes, had become involved in a fog bank, in the midst of which she now lay, with little or no wind to help her out of it.

Zac was not alone on board, nor had the present voyage been undertaken on his own account, or of his own motion. There were two passengers, one of whom had engaged the schooner for his own purposes. This one was a young fellow who called himself Claude Motier, of Randolph. His name, as well as his face, had a foreign character; yet he spoke English with the accent of an Englishman, and had been brought up in Massachusetts, near Boston, where he and Zac had seen very much of one another, on sea and on shore. The other passenger was a Roman Catholic priest, whose look and accent proclaimed him to be a Frenchman. He seemed about fifty years of age, and his bronzed faced, grizzled hair, and deeply-wrinkled brow, all showed the man of action rather than the recluse. Between these two passengers there was the widest possible difference. The one was almost a boy, the other a world-worn old man; the one full of life and vivacity, the other sombre and abstracted; yet between the two there was, however, a mysterious resemblance, which possibly may have been something more than that air of France, which they both had.

Whatever it may have been, they had been strangers to one another until the past few days, for Claude Motier had not seen the priest until after he had chartered the schooner for a voyage to Louisbourg. The priest had then come, asking for a passage to that port. He gave his name as the Abbé Michel, and addressed Claude in such bad English that the young man answered in French of the best sort, whereat the good priest seemed much delighted, and the two afterwards conversed with each other altogether in that language.

Besides these three, there were the ship's company dispersed about the vessel. This company were not very extensive, not numbering over three, in addition to Zac. These three all differed in age, in race, and in character. The aged colored man, who was at that moment washing out some tins at the bows, came aboard as cook, with the understanding that he was to be man of all work. He was a slave of Zac's, but, like many domestic slaves in those days, he seemed to regard himself as part of his master's family, — in fact, a sort of respected relative. He rejoiced in the name of Jericho, which was often shortened to Jerry, though the aged African considered the shorter name as a species of familiarity which was only to be tolerated on the part of his master. The second of the ship's company was a short, athletic, rosy-cheeked, bright-eyed, round-faced lad, who was always singing and dancing except when he was whistling. His name was Terry, and his country Ireland. In addition to Jerry and Terry, there was a third. He was a short, dull, and somewhat doleful looking boy of about twelve, who had a crushed expression, and seemed to take gloomy views of life. The only name by which he was known to himself and others was Biler; but whether that was a Christian name, or a surname, or a nickname, cannot be said. Biler's chief trouble in life was an inordinate and insatiable appetite. Nothing came amiss, and nothing was ever refused. Zac had picked the boy up three years before, and since that time he had never known him to be satisfied. At the present moment, Terry was standing at the tiller, while Biler was at the masthead, to which he had climbed to get rid of the disappointments of the world below, in a more elevated sphere, and from his lofty perch he was gazing with a hungry eye forth into space, and from time to time pulling bits of dried codfish from his pocket, and thrusting them into his mouth.

"Hy da!" suddenly shouted the aged Jericho, looking up. "You da, Biler? You jis come down heah an' help me fotch along dese yar tings. Ef you ain't got notin' to do, Ise precious soon find you lots ob tings. Hurry down, da; make haste; relse I'll pitch some hot water up at you. I can't be boddered wid dese yer pots an' pans any longer, cos Ise got de dinna to meditate 'bout."

With these words Jericho stood up, regarding Biler with an appearance of grave dignity, which would have overawed even a less solemn lad than this. Biler did not refuse obedience, but thrusting a few fragments of dried codfish into his mouth, heaved a sigh, gave another dejected look at surrounding space, and then slowly and mournfully descended to the lower world.

The priest was seated on a water-cask, reading his Breviary, while Zac stood not far off, looking thoughtfully over the vessel's side. Terry was at the tiller, not because there was any steering to be done, but because he thought it would be as well for every one to be at his post in the event of a change of wind.

He had whistled "St. Patrick's Day in the Morning," and was about beginning another interminable strain of the same kind. Claude was lounging about, and gradually drew nearer to the meditative Zac, whom he accosted.

"Well, we don't appear to be making much progress — do we?" said he.

Zac slowly shook his head.

"No," said he; "I must say, I don't like this here one mite. 'Tain't quite right. Seems kin' o' unlucky."

"Unlucky? How?"

"Wal, fust and foremost, ef it hadn't been you, you'd never a' got me to pint the Parson's nose for that French hole, Louisbourg."

"Why not?" asked Claude, in some surprise; "you don't suppose that there's any danger — do you?"

"Wal, it's a risky business — no doubt o' that thar. You see, my 'pinion is this, that Moosoo's my nat'ral born enemy, an' so I don't like to put myself into his power."

"O, there's no danger," said Claude, cheerily. "There's peace now, you know — as yet."

Zac shook his head.

"No," said he, "that ain't so. There ain't never real peace out here. There's on'y a kin' o' partial peace in the old country. Out here, we fight, an' we've got to go on fightin', till one or the other goes down. An' as to peace, 'tain't goin' to last long, even in the old country, 'cordin' to all accounts. There's fightin' already off in Germany, or somewhars, they say."

"But you know," said Claude, "you thought you

could manage this for me somehow. You said you could put me ashore somewhere without trusting yourself in Louisbourg harbor — some bay or other — wasn't it? I forget what the name is. There's no trouble about that now — is there?"

"Wal, not more'n thar was afore," said Zac, slowly; "on'y it seems more resky to me here, jest now, settin' here this way, inactive like; p'aps it's the fog that's had a kin' o' depressin' effect on my sperrits; it's often so. Or mebbe it's the effect of the continooal hearin' of that darned frog-eatin' French lingo that you go on a jabberin' with the priest thar. I never could abide it, nor my fathers afore me; an' how ever you — you, a good Protestant, an' a Massachusetts boy, an' a loyal subject of his most gracious majesty, King George — can go on that way, jabberin' all day long with that thar priest in that darned outlandish lingo, — wal, it beats me, — it doos clar."

At this Claude burst into a merry laugh.

"Well, by George," he cried, "if this ain't the greatest case of patriotic prejudice! What's the matter with the French language? It's better than English to talk with. Besides, even if it wern't, the French can't help their language. If it were yours, you'd like it, you know. And then I hope you're not beginning to take a prejudice against the good Père Michel. He's as fine a fellow as ever lived, by George!"

"O, mind you, now, I wan't intendin' to say anythin' agin him," said Zac. "I like him, an' can't help it, he's so gentle, an' meek, an' has sech a look out of his eyes. Blamed if I don't sometimes feel jest as though he's my father. O, no, I ain't got anythin' agin' him. Far from it. But it's the idee. For here, you see — this is the way it is; here aboard the Parson I see a Roman Catholic priest; I hear two people jabber French all day long. It makes me feel jest for all the world as though I'd got somehow into the hands of the Philistines. It seems like bein' a captive. It kin' o' seems a sort o' bad lookout; a kin' o' sort o' sign, you know, of what's a goin' to happen afore I git back agin."

At this, which was spoken with much earnestness, and with a very solemn face, Claude gave another laugh.

"O, that's all nonsense," said he, gayly. "Why, you don't really think, now, that you're going to get into trouble through me — do you? And then as to Père Michel, why, I feel as much confidence in him as I do in myself. So come, don't get into this low state of mind, but pluck up your spirits. Never mind the fog, or the French language. They oughtn't to have such an effect on a fellow of your size and general build. You'll put us ashore at that bay you spoke of, and then go home all right. That's the way of it. As to the land, you can't have any danger from that quarter; and as to the sea, why, you yourself said that the French cruiser was never built that could catch you."

"Wal," said Zac, "that's a fac', an' no mistake. Give me any kin' of wind, an' thar ain't a Moosoo afloat that can come anywhar nigh the Parson. Still, jest now, in this here fog, — an' in the calm, too, — if a Moosoo was to come along, why, I railly don't — quite — know — what — I could — railly do."

"The fog! O, in the fog you'll be all right enough, you know," said Claude.

"O, but that's the very thing I don't know," said Zac. "That thar pint's the very identical pint that I don't feel at all clear about, an' would like to have settled."

Claude said nothing for a few moments. He now began to notice in the face, the tone, and the manner of Zac something very different from usual — a certain uneasiness approaching to anxiety, which seemed to be founded on something which he had not yet disclosed.

"What do you mean?" he asked, rather gravely, suddenly dropping his air of light banter.

Zac drew a long breath.

"Wal," said he, "this here fog makes it very easy for a Moosoo to haul up alongside all of a sudden, an' ax you for your papers. An' what's more," he continued, dropping his voice to a lower tone, and stooping, to bring his mouth nearer to Claude's ear, "what's more, I don't know but what, at this very moment, there's a Moosoo railly an' truly a little mite nearer to us than I altogether keer for to hev him."

"What!" exclaimed Claude, with a start; "do you really think so? What! near us, here in this fog?"

"Railly an' truly," said Zac, solemnly, "that's my identical meanin' — jest it, exactly; an' 'tain't overly pleasant, no how. See here;" and Zac dropped his voice to still lower tones, and drew still nearer to Claude, as he continued — "see here, now; I'll tell you what happened jest now. As I was a standin' here, jest afore you come up, I thought I heerd voices out thar on the starboard quarter — voices —"

"Voices!" said Claude. "O, nonsense! Voices! How can there be voices out there? It must have been the water."

Wal," continued Zac, still speaking in a low tone, "that's the very thing I thought when I fust heerd 'em; I thought, too, it must be the water. But, if you jest take the trouble to examine, you'll find that thar ain't enough motion in the water to make any sound at all. 'Tain't as if thar was a puffin' of the wind an a dashin' of the waves. Thar ain't no wind an' no waves, unfort'nat'ly; so it seems beyond a doubt that it must either be actooal voices, or else somethin' supernat'ral. An' for my part I'd give somethin' for the wind to rise jest a leetle mite, so's I could step off out o' this, an' git out o' hearin', at least."

At this Claude was again silent for some time, thinking to himself whether the possibility of a French ship being near was to be wished or dreaded. Much was to be said on both sides. To himself it would, perhaps, be desirable; yet not so to Zac, although he tried to reassure the dejected skipper by telling him that if a French vessel should really be so near, it would be all the better, since his voyage would thereby be made all the shorter, for he himself could go aboard, and the Parson might return to Boston. But Zac refused to be so easily comforted.

"No," said he; "once I git into their clutches, they'll never let me go; and as for the poor old Parson, why, they'll go an' turn her into a Papist priest. And that," he added, with a deep sigh, "would be too — almighty — bad!"

Claude now found that Zac was in too despondent a mood to listen to what he called reason, and therefore he held his tongue. The idea that a French ship might be somewhere near, behind that wall of fog, had in it something which to him was not unpleasant, since

2

it afforded some variety to the monotony of his situation. He stood, therefore, in silence, with his face turned towards the direction indicated by Zac, and listened intently, while the skipper stood in silence by his side, listening also.

There was no wind whatever. The water was quite smooth, and the Parson rose and fell at the slow undulations of the long ocean rollers, while at every motion the spars creaked and the sails flapped idly. All around there arose a gray wall of fog, deep, dense, and fixed, which shut them in on every side, while overhead the sky itself was concealed from view by the same dull-gray canopy. Behind that wall of fog anything might lie concealed; the whole French fleet might be there, without those on board the Parson being anything the wiser. This Claude felt, and as he thought of the possibility of this, he began to see that Zac's anxiety was very well founded, and that if the Parson should be captured it would be no easy task to deliver her from the grasp of the captor. Still there came no further sounds, and Claude, after listening for a long time without hearing anything, began, at length, to conclude that Zac had been deceived.

"Don't you think," he asked, "that it may, after all, have been the rustle of the sails, or the creaking of the spars?"

Zac shook his head.

"No," said he; "I've heerd it twice; an' I know very well all the sounds that sails an' spars can make; an' I don't see as how I can be mistook. O, no; it was human voice, an' nothin' else in natur'. I wouldn't mind it a mite if I could do anythin'. But to set here an' jest git caught, like a rat in a trap, is what I call too — almighty — bad!"

At this very instant, and while Zac was yet speaking, there came through the fog the sound of a voice. Claude heard it, and Zac also. The latter grasped the arm of his friend, and held his breath. It was a human voice. There was not the slightest doubt now of that. Words had been spoken, but they were unintelligible. They listened still. There was silence for a few moments, and then the silence was broken once more. Words were again heard. They were French, and they heard them this time with perfect distinctness. They were these: —

"*Put her head a little over this way.*"

CHAPTER II.

A MEETING IN MID OCEAN.

PUT *her head a little over this way!*

They were French words. To Claude, of course, they were perfectly intelligible, though not so to Zac, who did not understand any language but his mother Yankee. Judging by the distinctness and the loudness of the sound, the speaker could not be very far away. The voice seemed to come from the water astern. No sight, however, was visible; and the two, as they stared into the fog, saw nothing whatever. Nor did any of the others on board seem to have heard the voice. The priest was still intent on his Breviary. Terry was still whistling his abominable tune. Jericho was below with his pots and pans; and Biler, taking advantage of his absence, was seated on the taffrail devouring a raw turnip, which he chewed with a melancholy air. To none of these had the voice been audible, and therefore Claude and Zac alone were confronted with this mystery of the deep. But it was a mystery which they could not fathom; for the fog was all around, hiding everything from view, and the more they peered into the gloom the less were they able to understand it.

Neither of them spoke for some time. Zac had not understood the words, but was more puzzled about the fact of a speaker being so near on the water, behind the fog, than he was about the meaning of the words which had been spoken. That seemed to be quite a secondary consideration. And it was not until he had exhausted his resources in trying to imagine what or where the one might be, that he thought of asking about the other.

"What did it mean?" he asked, at length.

Claude told him.

Zac said nothing for some time.

"I wonder whether they've seen us," said he, at length. "No — 'tain't possible. The fog's too thick — and we're as invisible to them as they are to us. Besides, these words show that they ain't thinkin' about anybody but themselves. Well, all we've got to do is to keep as still as a mouse, an' I'll jest go an' warn the boys."

With these words Zac moved softly away to warn his crew. First he went to Terry, and informed him that the whole fleet of France was around the Parson, and that their only chance of safety was to keep silent — a piece of information which effectually stopped Terry's singing and whistling for some time; then he told Biler, in a friendly way, that if he spoke above a whisper, or made any noise, he'd pitch him overboard with an anchor tied to his neck. Then he warned Jericho. As for Père Michel, he felt that warning was unnecessary, for the priest was too absorbed in his book to be conscious of the external world. After this, he came back to Claude, who had been listening ever since he left, but without hearing anything more.

"We must have drifted nearer together," said Zac. "The voice was a good deal louder than when I fust heerd it. My only hope is, that they'll drift past us, an' we'll git further away from them. But I wonder what they meant by bringin' her head round. P'aps they've seen us, after all — an' then, again, p'aps they haven't."

He said this in a whisper, and Claude answered in another whisper.

"It seems to me," said Claude, "that if they'd seen us, they'd have said something more — or, at any rate, they'd have made more noise. But as it is, they've been perfectly silent."

"Wal — I on'y hope we won't hear anythin' more of them."

For more than two hours silence was observed on board the Parson. Terry stopped all whistling, and occupied himself with scratching his bullet head. The priest sat motionless, reading his book. Jericho drew the unhappy Biler down below for safe keeping, and detained him there a melancholy prisoner. Claude and Zac stood listening, but nothing more was heard.

To Claude there seemed something weird and ghostly in this incident — a voice thus sounding suddenly forth out of nothingness, and then dying away into the silence from which it had emerged: there was that in it which made him feel a sensation of involuntary awe; and the longer the silence continued, the more did this incident surround itself with a certain supernatural element, until, at length, he began to fancy that his senses might have deceived him. Yet he knew that this had not been the case. Zac had heard the voice as well as he, and the words to him had been perfectly plain. *Put her head a little over this way!* Singular words, too, they seemed to be, as he turned them over in his mind. Under other circumstances they might have been regarded as perfectly commonplace, but now the surroundings gave them the possibility of a varied interpretation. Who was the "her"? What was meant? Was it a ship, or a woman? What could the meaning be? Or, again, might not this have been some supernatural voice speaking to them from the Unseen, and conveying to them some sentence either of good or of evil omen, giving them some direction, perhaps, about the course of the schooner in which he was?

Not that Claude was what is called a superstitious man. From ordinary superstition he was, indeed, quite as free as any man of his age or epoch; nor was he even influenced by any of the common superstitious fancies then prevalent. But still there is a natural belief in the unseen which prevails among all men, and Claude's fancy was busy, being stimulated by this incident, so that, as he endeavored to account for it, he was as easily drawn towards a supernatural theory as to a natural one. Hundreds of miles from land, on the broad ocean, a voice had sounded from behind the impenetrable cloud, and it was scarcely to be wondered at that he considered it something unearthly.

Under other circumstances Zac might also have yielded to superstitious fancies; but as it was, his mind had been too completely filled with the one absorbing idea of the French fleet to find room for any other thought. It was not an unsubstantial ghost which Zac dreaded, but the too substantial form of some frigate looming through the fog, and firing a gun to bring him on board. Every additional moment of silence gave him a feeling of relief, for he felt that

About a week before this the Arethuse had encountered a severe gale, accompanied by a dense fog, in which they had lost their reckoning. To add to their miseries, they found themselves surrounded by icebergs, among which navigation was so difficult that the seamen all became demoralized. At length the ship struck one of these floating masses, and instantly began to fill. The desperate efforts of the crew, however, served to keep her afloat for another day, and might have saved her, had it not been for the continuation of the fog. On the following night, in the midst of intense darkness, she once more struck against an iceberg, and this time the consequences were more serious. A huge fragment of ice fell upon the poop, shattering it and sweeping it overboard. In an instant all discipline was at an end. It was *sauve qui peut.* The crew took to the boats. One of these went down with all on board, while the others passed away into the darkness. This little handful had thrown themselves upon the ship's poop, which was floating alongside within reach, just in time to escape being dragged down by the sinking ship; and there, for days and nights, with scarcely any food, and no shelter whatever, they had drifted amid the dense fog, until all hope had died out utterly. Such had been their situation when rescue came.

Claude, upon hearing this story, expressed a sympathy which was most sincere; and to the seamen it was all the pleasanter as his accent showed him to be a countryman. But the general sympathy which the young man felt, sincere though it was, could not be compared with that special sympathy which he experienced for the lovely young girl whom he had borne from the raft into the schooner, and whose deep glance of speechless gratitude had never since faded from his memory. She was now aboard, and was occupying his own room. More than this, she had already taken up a position within his mind which was a pre-eminent one. She had driven out every thought of everything else. The highest desire which he had was to see once again that face which had become so vividly impressed upon his memory, and find out what it might be like in less anxious moments. But for this he would have to wait.

Meanwhile the schooner had resumed her voyage, in which, however, she made but slow progress. The wind, which had come up so opportunely, died out again; and, though the fog had gone, still for a few days they did little else than drift.

After the first day and night the Count de Laborde came upon deck. He was extremely feeble, and had great difficulty in walking; with him were his daughter and her maid. Although her exhaustion and prostration on the raft had, apparently, been even greater than his, yet youth was on her side, and she had been able to rally much more rapidly. She and her maid supported the feeble old count, and anxiously anticipated his wants with the fondest care.

Claude had hoped for this appearance, and was not disappointed. He had seen her first as she was emerging from the valley of the shadow of death, with the stamp of sorrow and despair upon her features; but now no trace of despair remained; her face was sweet and joyous beyond expression, with the grace of a child-like innocence and purity. The other passenger, whom the lieutenant of the Arethuse had called the Count de Cazeneau, was also on deck, and, on seeing Laborde and his daughter, he hastened towards them with the utmost fervor of congratulations. The lieutenant also went to pay his respects. The young countess was most gracious, thanking them for their good wishes, and assuring them that she was as well as ever; and then her eyes wandered away, and, after a brief interval, at length rested with a fixed and earnest look full upon Claude. The glance thrilled through him. For a moment he stood as if fixed to the spot; but at length, mastering his emotion, he went towards her.

"Here he is, papa, dearest," said she, — "our noble deliverer. — And, O, monsieur, how can we ever find words to thank you?"

"Dear monsieur," said the old count, embracing Claude, "Heaven will reward you; our words are useless. — Mimi," he continued, turning to his daughter, "your dream was a true one. — You must know, monsieur, that she dreamed that a young Frenchman came in an open boat to save us. And so it really was."

Mimi smiled and blushed.

"Ah, papa, dear," she said, "I dreamed because I hoped. I always hoped, but you always desponded. And now it has been better than our hopes. — But, monsieur, may we not know the name of our deliverer?"

She held out her little hand as she said this. Claude raised it respectfully to his lips, bowing low as he did so. He then gave his name, but hastened to assure them that he was not their preserver, insisting that Zac had the better claim to that title. To this, however, the others listened with polite incredulity, and

Mimi evidently considered it all the mere expression of a young man's modesty. She waved her little hand with a sunny smile.

"*Eh bien*," she said, "I see, monsieur, it pains you to have people too grateful; so we will say no more about it. We must satisfy ourselves by remembering and by praying."

Here the conversation was interrupted by the interposition of the Count de Cazeneau, who came forward to add his thanks to those of Laborde. He made a little set speech, to which Claude listened with something of chagrin, for he did not like being placed in the position of general savior and preserver, when he knew that Zac deserved quite as much credit for what had been done as he did. This was not unobserved by Mimi, who appreciated his feelings and came to his relief.

"M. Motier does not like being praised," said she. "Let us respect his delicacy."

But Cazeneau was not to be stopped so easily. He seemed like one who had prepared a speech carefully and with much labor, and was, accordingly, bound to give it all; so Claude was forced to listen to an eloquent and inflated panegyric about himself and his heroism, without being able to offer anything more than an occasional modest disclaimer. And all the time the deep, dark glance of Mimi was fixed on him, as though she would read his soul. If, indeed, she had any skill in reading character, it was easy enough to see in the face of that young man a pure, a lofty, and a generous nature, unsullied by anything mean or low, a guileless and earnest heart, a soul *sans peur et sans reproche;* and it did seem by the expression of her own face as though she had read all this in Claude.

Further conversation of a general nature followed, which served to explain the position of all of them with reference to one another. Claude was the virtual master of the schooner, since he had chartered it for his own purposes. To all of them, therefore, he seemed first their savior, and secondly their host and entertainer, to whom they were bound to feel chiefly grateful. Yet none the less did they endeavor to include the honest skipper in their gratitude; and Zac came in for a large share of it. Though he could not understand any of the words which they addressed to him, yet he was easily able to guess what they were driving at, and so he modestly disclaimed it all with the expression, —

"O, sho! sho, now! sho, sho!"

They now learned that Claude was on his way to Louisbourg, and that they would thus be able to reach their original destination. They also learned the circumstances of Zac, and his peculiar unwillingness to trust his schooner inside the harbor of Louisbourg. Zac's scruples were respected by them, though they all declared that there was no real danger. They were sufficiently satisfied to be able to reach any point near Louisbourg, and did not seek to press Zac against his will, or to change his opinion upon a point where it was so strongly expressed.

No sooner had these new passengers thus unexpectedly appeared, than a very marked change came over Père Michel, which to Claude was quite inexplicable. To him and to Zac the good priest had thus far seemed everything that was most amiable and companionable;

but now, ever since the moment when he had turned away at the sight of the face of Laborde, he had grown strangely silent, and reticent, and self-absorbed. Old Laborde had made advances which had been coldly repelled. Cazeneau, also, had tried to draw him out, but without success. To the lieutenant only was he at all inclined to unbend. Yet this strange reserve did not last long; and at length Père Michel regained his old manner, and received the advances of Laborde with sufficient courtesy, while to Mimi he showed that paternal gentleness which had already endeared him to Claude and to Zac.

Several days thus passed, during which but little progress was made. The schooner seemed rather to drift than to sail. Whenever a slight breeze would arise, it was sure to be adverse, and was not of long duration. Then a calm would follow, and the schooner would lie idle upon the bosom of the deep.

During these days Mimi steadily regained her strength; and the bloom and the sprightliness of youth came back, and the roses began to return to her cheeks, and her wan face resumed its plumpness, and her eyes shone with the light of joyousness. Within the narrow confines of a small schooner, Claude was thrown in her way more frequently than could have been the case under other circumstances; and the situation in which they were placed towards one another connected them more closely, and formed a bond which made an easy way to friendship, and even intimacy. As a matter of course, Claude found her society pleasanter by far than that of any one else on board; while, on the other hand, Mimi did not seem at all averse to his companionship. She seemed desirous to know all about him.

"But, monsieur," she said once, in the course of a conversation, "it seems strange to me that you have lived so long among the English here in America."

"It is strange," said Claude; "and, to tell the truth, I don't altogether understand myself how it has happened."

"Ah, you don't understand yourself how it has happened," repeated Mimi, in a tone of voice that was evidently intended to elicit further confidences.

"No," said Claude, who was not at all unwilling to receive her as his confidante. "You see I was taken away from France when I was an infant."

"When you were an infant!" said Mimi. "How very, very sad!" and saying this, she turned her eyes, with a look full of deepest commiseration, upon him. "And so, of course, you cannot remember anything at all about France."

Claude shook his head.

"No, nothing at all," said he. "But I'm on my way there now; and I hope to see it before long. It's the most beautiful country in all the world — isn't it?'

"Beautiful!" exclaimed Mimi, throwing up her eyes; "there are no words to describe it. It is heaven! Alas! how can I ever bear to live here in this wild and savage wilderness of America!"

"You did not wish to leave France then?" said Claude, who felt touched by this display of feeling.

"I!" exclaimed Mimi; "I wish to leave France! Alas, monsieur! it was the very saddest day of all my life. But dear papa had to go, and I do not know why it was. He offered to let me stay; but I could not let him go alone, for he is so old and feeble, and I was willing to endure all for his sake."

"What part of France did you live in?" asked Claude.

"Versailles."

"That is where the court is," said Claude.

"Of course," said Mimi, with a smile. "But how funny it seems to hear a Frenchman make such a remark, and in such an uncertain way, as though he did not feel quite sure. Why, monsieur, in France Versailles is everything; Versailles is the king and court. In a word, monsieur, Versailles is France."

"I suppose you saw very much of the splendor and magnificence of the court?" said Claude.

"I!" said Mimi; "splendor and magnificence! the court! *Ma foi*, monsieur, I did not see any of it at all. In France young girls are kept close-guarded. You have lived among the English, and among them I have heard that young girls can go anywhere and do anything. But for my part I have always lived most secluded — sometimes at school, and afterwards at home."

"How strange it is," said Claude, "that your father should leave France, when he is so old and feeble, and take you, too, and come to this wild country!"

"O, it is very strange," said Mimi, "and very sad; and I don't know why in the world it was, for he will never tell me. Sometimes I think that something unfortunate has happened, which has made him go into exile this way. But then, if that were so, I don't see why he should remain in French possessions. If his political enemies have driven him away, he would not be safe in French colonies; and so I don't know why in the world he ever left home."

"Does he intend to remain at Louisbourg, or go farther?" asked Claude, after a thoughtful pause.

"I'm sure I don't know," said Mimi; "but I don't think he has decided yet. It is just as if he was looking for something, and as if he would travel about till he found it; though what it is that he wants I can hardly tell. And such, monsieur, is our mournful position. We may remain at Louisbourg a short time or a long time: it depends upon circumstances. We may go to Quebec, or even to New Orleans."

"New Orleans!" exclaimed Claude.

"Yes; I heard him hint as much. And he said, also, that if he did go as far as that, he would leave me at Quebec or Louisbourg. But I will never consent to that, and I will go with him wherever he goes."

"I should think that such a roving life would make you feel very unhappy."

"O, no; I am not unhappy," said Mimi, cheerfully. "I should, indeed, feel unhappy if I were left behind in France, or anywhere else, and if poor papa should go roaming about without any one to care for him. I am not much; but I know that he loves me dearly, and that he is very much happier with me than without me. And that is the reason why I am determined to go with him wherever he goes,— yes, even if he goes among the savages. Besides, while I am with him, he has a certain amount of anxiety about me, and this distracts his thoughts, and prevents him from brooding too much over his own personal troubles. But O, how I envy you, Monsieur Motier, and O, how I should love to be going back to France, if dear papa were only going there too! I shall never be happy again, I know, never, till I am back again in France."

CHAPTER IV.

MIMI AND MARGOT.

WHILE Claude was doing the honors of hospitality to the guests aft, the crew of the Parson was fraternizing with the seamen of the wrecked Arethuse, forward. The first and most important act of friendly intercourse was the work of Jericho, who put forth all his skill in preparing for the half-starved sailors a series of repasts upon which he lavished all his genius, together with the greater part of the stores of the schooner. To these repasts the seamen did ample justice, wasting but little time in unnecessary words, but eating as only those can eat who have been on the borders of starvation. Yet it may be questioned whether their voracity exceeded that of a certain melancholy boy, who waited on the banquet, and whose appetite seemed now even more insatiable in the midst of the abundant supplies which Jericho produced, than it had been in former days, when eatables had been less choice and repasts less frequent. In fact, Biler outdid himself, and completely wore out the patience of the long-suffering Jericho.

"You jes look heah, you Biler," he said; "you better mind, for I ain't goin' to stand dese yer goins on no longer. Dar's limits to eberyting — and dese yer 'visiums has got to be 'commonized, an' not to be all gobbled up by one small boy. Tell you what, I got a great mind to put you on a lowns, an' gib you one rore turnip a day, an' ef you can ketch a fish I'll 'gree to cook it. Why, dar ain't de vessel afloat dat can stand dis yer. You eat fifty-nine meals a day, an' more. You nebber do notin' else but eat — morn', noon, an' night."

"Arrah, Jerry, let the b'y ate his fill," said Terry: "sure an' a growin' b'y has to ate more'n a grown man, so as to get flesh to grow wid."

"Can't do it," said Jerry, "an' won't do it. Didn't mind it so much afore, but now we'se got to 'commonize. Dar's ebber so many more moufs aboard now, an' all on 'em eat like sin. Dis yer calm keeps us out heah in one spot, an' when we're ebber a goin' to get to de end ov de vyge's more'n I can tell. No use frowin' away our val'ble 'visiums on dis yer boy — make him eat soap fat and oakum — good enough for him. No 'casium for him to be eatin' a hundred times more'n all de res ob us. If he wants to eat he'll hab to find his own 'visiums, an' ketch a shark, an' I'll put it in pickle for he own private use."

With these words Jericho turned away with deep trouble and perplexity visible on his ebon brow, and Biler, pocketing a few potatoes and turnips, climbed to the mast-head, where he sat gazing in a melancholy way into space.

To Terry these new comers were most welcome. At a distance he professed to hate and despise the French; but now that they appeared face to face, his hate was nowhere, and in its place there was nothing but a most earnest desire to form an eternal friendship with the shipwrecked seamen. There was certainly one difficulty in the way which was of no slight character; and that was, that neither of them knew the language of the other. But Terry was not easily daunted, and the very presence of a difficulty was enough to make him feel eager to triumph over it.

In his first approaches he made the very common mistake of addressing the French sailors as though they were deaf. Thus he went up to them one after the other, shaking hands with each, and shouting in their ears as loud as he could, "*How do yez do?*" "*Good day.*" "*The top av the mornin' to yez.*" To which the good-natured Frenchmen responded in a sympathetic way, shaking his hand vigorously, and grinning and chattering. Terry kept this up for some time; but at length it became somewhat monotonous, and he set his wits to work to try to discover some more satisfactory mode of effecting a communication with them. The next way that he thought of was something like the first, and, like the first, is also frequently resorted to by those who have occasion to speak to foreigners. It was to address them in broken English, or rather in a species of baby talk; for to Terry it seemed no more than natural that this sort of dialect would be more intelligible than the speech of full-grown men.

Accordingly, as soon as Terry thought of this, he put it in practice. He began by shaking hands once more, and then said to them, "Me berry glad see you — me sposy you berry hundy. Polly want a cracker. He sall hab penty mate den, so he sall. Did de naughty water boos um den?"

But unfortunately this effort proved as much of a failure as the other; so Terry was once more compelled to trust to his wits. Those wits of his, being active, did not fail, indeed, to suggest many ways, and of the best kind, by which he brought himself into communication with his new friends. At the first repast he found this out, and insisted upon passing everything to them with his own hands, accompanying each friendly offer with an affectionate smile, which went straight to the hearts of the forlorn and half-starved guests. This was a language which was every way intelligible, the language of universal humanity, in which the noblest precept is, to be kind to enemies and to feed the hungry.

In addition to this, Terry also found out other ways of holding communication with them, the chief of which was by the language of song. Terry's irrepressible tendency to singing thus burst forth in their presence, and after trolling out a few Irish melodies, he succeeded in eliciting from them a sympathetic response in the shape of some lively French songs. The result proved most delightful to all concerned; and thereafter the muse of Ireland and the muse of France kept up a perpetual antiphonal song, which beguiled many a tedious hour.

While the various characters on board the schooner were thus entering into communication with one another, Zac endeavored also to scrape an acquaintance with one of the rescued party, who seemed to him to be worth all the rest put together. This was Mimi's maid, Margot, a beautiful little creature, full of life and spirit, and fit companion for such a mistress as hers. The good little Margot was very accessible, and had not failed to pour forth in language not very intelligible her sense of gratitude to Zac. She had not forgotten that it was Zac who had conveyed her in his strong arms from death to life, and therefore persisted in regarding him not only as the preserver of her own self, but as the real and only preserver of all the others.

Margot had one advantage which was delightful to Zac; and that was, she could speak a little English. She had once spent a year in England, where she had picked up enough of the language to come and go upon, and this knowledge now proved to be of very great advantage.

The calm weather which continued gave Zac many opportunities of drifting away towards Margot, and talking with her, in which talks they gradually grew to be better acquainted.

"I am so happy zat I spik Ingelis!" said Margot; "I nevar did sink dat it was evare useful."

"An' pooty blamed lucky it's ben for me, too," said Zac, in a joyous tone; "for as I don't know French, like Claude over there, I have to trust to you to keep up the conversation."

"I not know mooch Ingelis," said Margot, "for I not understan de mooch of what you say."

"O, you'll learn dreadful fast out here," said Zac.

"But I not weesh to stay here so long as to learn," said Margot.

"Not wish! Sho, now! Why, it's a better country than France."

"Than France — better!" cried Margot, lifting her hands and throwing up her eyes in amazement. "France! Monsieur, France is a heaven — mais — dees — dees — is different."

"Why, what's the matter with America?" said Zac.

"Amérique — eet ees all full of de sauvage — de Indian — de wild men — an' wild beasts — an' desert."

"O, you ain't ben to Boston; that's clar," said Zac, mildly. "Jest you wait till you see Boston; that's all."

"Boston! I nevare hear of Boston," said Margot, "till you tell me. I do not believe eet it is more magnifique dan Paris."

"The most magnificent town in the hull world," said Zac, calmly. "You take the House of Assembly an' Govement House — take King Street and Queen Street, an' I'd like to know whar you'll find a better show any whar on airth."

"Sais pas," said Margot; "nevare see Boston. Mais vous — you nevare see Paris — so we are not able to compare."

"O, well, it's nat'ral enough for you," said Zac, with magnanimity, "nat'ral enough for you, course, to like your own place best — 'twouldn't be nat'ral ef you didn't. All your friends live thar, course. You were born thar, and I s'pose your pa an' ma may be there now, anxiously expectin' to hear from you."

Zac put this in an interrogative way, for he wanted to know. But as he said these words, the smiling face of Margot turned sad; she shook her head, and said, —

"No; I have no one, no one!"

"What! no relatives!" said Zac, in a voice full of commiseration and tender pity.

Margot shook her head.

"An' so you've got no father nor mother, an' you're a poor little orphan girl!" said Zac, in a broken voice.

Margot shook her head, and looked sadder than ever.

Tears came to Zac's eyes. He felt as he had never felt before. There was something so inexpressibly touching about this orphan! He took her little hand tenderly in his own great, brown, toil-worn fist, and looked at her very wistfully. For a few moments he said nothing. Margot looked up at him with her great brown eyes, and then looked meekly at the deck. Zac heaved a deep sigh; then he placed his disengaged hand solemnly upon her head.

"Wal," said he, gravely, "I'll protect you. Ef anybody ever harms you, you jest come to me. I'll — I'll be — a father to you."

Again Margot looked up at him with her great brown eyes.

"O, dat's noting," she said. "I don't want you to be my fader. But, all de same, I tink you one very nice man; an' you safe my life; an' I sall not forget — nevare; an' I weesh—. Sall I tell you what I weesh?"

"Yes, yes," said Zac, eagerly, with a strange thrill of excitement.

Margot threw a quick look around.

"Dees Monsieur de Cazeneau," said she, drawing nearer to Zac, and speaking in a low, quick voice, "I 'fraid of heem. Dere is danjaire for my mademoiselle. He is a bad man. He haf a plot — a plan. You moos safe us. Dees Monsieur Motier is no good. You haf safe us from death; you moos safe us from dees danjaire."

"How?" asked Zac, who took in at once the meaning of Margot's words, though not fully understanding them.

"I will tell. Dess Monsieur de Cazeneau wish to

get us to Louisbourg, where he will ruin us all — dat is, de ole count and de mademoiselle. You moos turn about, and take us to Boston."

"Take you to Boston! But this schooner is engaged to go to Louisbourg with Mr. Motier."

Margot shook her head.

"You moos do it," said she, "or we sall be ruin. You moos tell Monsieur Motier—"

Zac now began questioniong her further; but Margot could not remain any longer; she therefore hurried away, with the promise to see him again and explain more about it; and Zac was left alone with his own thoughts, not knowing exactly what he could say to Claude, or how he could make up, out of Margot's scanty information, a story which might offer sufficient ground for a change in the purpose of the voyage.

Meanwhile Claude had seen Mimi at various times, and had conversed with her, as before, in a very confidential manner. The danger of which Margot had spoken was present in Mimi's thoughts, also; and she was anxious to secure Claude's assistance.

Thus it was that Mimi communicated to Claude all about her personal affairs. There was something almost childish in this ready communicativeness; but she knew no reason for concealing anything, and therefore was thus frank and outspoken. Claude, also, was quite as willing to tell all about himself; though his own story was somewhat more involved, and could not be told piecemeal, but required a longer and more elaborate explanation.

"Have you many friends in France?" asked Mimi, in an abrupt sort of way, the next time they met.

"Friends in France?" repeated Claude; "not one, that I know of."

"No friends! Then what can you do there?" she asked, innocently.

"Well, I don't know yet," said he. "I will see when I get there. The fact is, I am going there to find out something about my own family — my parents and myself."

At this Mimi fastened her large eyes upon Claude with intense interest.

"How strangely you talk!" said she.

"I'll tell you a secret," said Claude, after a pause.

"What?" she asked.

"You will never tell it to any one? It's very important."

"I tell it?" repeated Mimi; "I! Never. Of course not. So, now, what is the secret?"

"Well, it's this: my name is not Motier."

"Well," said Mimi, "I'm sure I'm very glad that it isn't; and it seemed strange when you told me first, for Motier is a plebeian name; and you certainly are no plebeian."

"I am not a plebeian," said Claude, proudly. "You are right. My name is one of the noblest in France. I wonder if you can tell me what I want to know!"

"I! Why, how can I?" said Mimi. "But I should so like to know what it is that you want to know! And O, monsieur, I should so love to know what is your real name and family!"

"Well," said Claude, "I don't as yet know much about it myself. But I do know what my real name is. I am the Count de Montresor."

"Montresor," exclaimed Mimi, "Montresor!"

As she said this, there was an evident agitation in her voice and manner which did not escape Claude.

"What's the matter?" said he. "You know something. Tell me what it is! O, tell me!"

Mimi looked at him very earnestly.

"I don't know," said she; "I don't know anything at all. I only know this, that poor papa's troubles are connected in some way with some one whose name is Montresor. But his troubles are a thing that I am afraid to speak about, and therefore I have never found out anything about them. So I don't know anything about Montresor, more than this. And the trouble is something terrible, I know," continued Mimi, "for it has forced him, at his time of life, to leave his home and become an exile. And I'm afraid — that is, I imagine — that he himself has done some wrong in his early life to some Montresor. But I'm afraid to ask him; and I think now that the sole object of his journey is to atone for this wrong that he has done. And O, monsieur, now that you tell your name, now that you say how you have been living here all your life, I have a fearful suspicion that my papa has been the cause of it. Montresor! How strange!"

Mimi was very much agitated; so much so, indeed, that Claude repented having told her this. But it was now too late to repent, and he could only try to find some way of remedying the evil.

"Suppose I go to your father," said he, "and tell him who I am, and all about myself."

"No, no," cried Mimi, earnestly; "do not! O, do not! I would not have you for worlds. My hope is, that he may give up his search and go home again, and find peace. There is nothing that you can do. What it is that troubles him I don't know; but it was something that took place before you or I were born

— many, many years ago. You can do nothing. You would only trouble him the more. If he has done wrong to you or yours, you would only make his remorse the worse, for he would see in you one whom his acts have made an exile."

"O, nonsense!" said Claude, cheerily; "I haven't been anything of the kind. For my part, I've lived a very happy life indeed; and it's only of late that I found out my real name. I'll tell you all about it some time, and then you'll understand better. As to anybody feeling remorse about my life, that's all nonsense. I consider my life rather an enviable one thus far."

At this Mimi's agitation left her, and she grew calm again. She looked at Claude with a glance of deep gratitude, and said,—

"O, how glad, how very glad, I am to hear you say that! Perhaps you may be able yet to tell that to my dear papa. But still, I do not wish you to say anything to him at all till I may find some time when you may do it safely. And you will promise me — will you not? — that you will keep this a secret from him till he is able to bear it."

"Promise? Of course," said Claude.

She held out her hand, and Claude took it and carried it to his lips. They had been sitting at the bows of the schooner during this conversation. No one was near, and they had been undisturbed.

CHAPTER V.

A STRANGE REVELATION.

THE old Count Laborde had been too much weakened by suffering and privation to recover very rapidly. For a few days he spent most of his time reclining upon a couch in the little cabin, where Mimi devoted herself to him with the tenderest care. At times she would come upon deck at the urgent request of her father, and then Claude would devote himself to her with still more tender care. The old man did not take much notice of surrounding things. He lay most of the time with his eyes closed, in a half-dreamy state, and it was only with an effort that he was able to rouse himself to speak. He took no notice whatever of any one but his daughter. Cazeneau made several efforts to engage his attention, but he could not be roused.

Thus there were short intervals, on successive days, when Claude was able to devote himself to Mimi, for the laudable purpose of beguiling the time which he thought must hang heavy on her hands. He considered that as he was in some sort the master of the schooner, these strangers were all his guests, and he was therefore bound by the sacred laws of hospitality to make it as pleasant for them as possible. Of course, also, it was necessary that he should exert his hospitable powers most chiefly for the benefit of the lady; and this necessity he followed up with very great spirit and assiduity.

By the conversation which he had already had with her, it will be seen that they had made rapid advances towards intimacy. Claude was eager to extend this advance still farther, to take her still more into his confidence, and induce her to take him into hers. He was very eager to tell her all about himself, and the nature of his present voyage; he was still more eager to learn from her all that she might know about the Montresor family. And thus he was ever on the lookout for her appearance on deck.

These appearances were not so frequent as he desired; but Mimi's devotion to her father kept her below most of the time. At such times Claude did the agreeable to the other passengers, with varying success. With the lieutenant he succeeded in ingratiating himself very rapidly; but with Cazeneau all his efforts proved futile. There was about this man a sullen reserve and *hauteur* which made conversation difficult and friendship impossible. Claude was full of *bonhomie*, good-nature generally, and sociability; but Cazeneau was more than he could endure; so that, after a few attempts, he retired, baffled, vexed at what he considered the other's aristocratic pride. What was more noticed by him now, was the fact that Père Michel had grown more reserved with him; not that there was any visible change in the good priest's friendly manner, but he seemed pre-occupied and strangely self-absorbed. And so things went on.

Meantime the schooner can hardly be said to have

gone on at all. What with light head winds, and currents, and calms, her progress was but slow. This state of things was very irritating to Zac, who began to mutter something about these rascally Moosoos bringing bad luck, and "he'd be darned if he wouldn't like to know where in blamenation it was all going to end." But as Claude was no longer so good a listener as he used to be, Zac grew tired of talking to empty space, and finally held his peace. The winds and tides, and the delay, however, made no difference with Claude, nor did it interfere in the slightest with his self-content and self-complacency. In fact, he looked as though he rather enjoyed the situation; and this was not the least aggravating thing in the surroundings to the mind of the impatient skipper.

Thus several days passed, and at length Claude had an opportunity of drawing Mimi into another somewhat protracted conversation.

"I am very much obliged to you," said Claude, gayly, "for making your appearance. I have been trying to do the agreeable to your shipmate Cazeneau, but without success. Is he always so amiable? and is he a friend of yours?"

Mimi looked at Claude with a very serious expression as he said this, and was silent for a few minutes.

"He is a friend of papa's," said she at last. "He came out with us —"

"Is he a great friend of yours?" asked Claude.

Mimi hesitated for a moment, and then said, —

"No; I do not like him at all."

Claude drew a long breath.

"Nor do I," said he.

"Perhaps I am doing him injustice," said Mimi,

"but I cannot help feeling as though he is in some way connected with dear papa's troubles. I do not mean to say that he is the cause of them. I merely mean that, as far as I know anything about them, it is always in such a way that he seems mixed up with them. And I don't think, either, that his face is very much in his favor, for there is something so harsh and cruel in his expression, that I always wish that papa had chosen some different kind of a person for his friend and confidant."

"Is he all that?" asked Claude.

"O, I suppose so," said Mimi. "They have secrets together, and make, together, plans that I know nothing about."

"Do you suppose," asked Claude, "that you will ever be in any way connected with their plans?"

He put this question, which was a general one, in a very peculiar tone, which indicated some deeper meaning. It seemed as though Mimi understood him, for she threw at him a hurried and half-frightened look.

"Why?" she asked. "What makes you ask such a question as that?"

"O, I don't know," said Claude. "The thought merely entered my mind — perhaps because I dislike him, and suspect him, and am ready to imagine all kinds of evil about him."

Mimi regarded him now with a very earnest look, and said nothing for some time.

"Have you any recollection," she asked, at length, "of ever having seen his face anywhere, at any time, very long ago?"

Claude shook his head.

"Not the slightest," said he. "I never saw him in

all my life, or any one like him, till I saw him on the raft. But what makes you ask so strange a question?"

"I hardly know," said Mimi, "except that he seems so in papa's confidence, — and I know that papa's chief trouble arises from some affair that he had with some Montresor, — and I thought — well, I'll tell you what I thought. I thought that, as this Montresor had to leave France — that perhaps he had been followed to America, or sought after; and, as you are a member of that family, you might have seen some of those who were watching the family; and the Count de Cazeneau seemed to be one who might be connected with it. But I'm afraid I'm speaking in rather a confused way; and no wonder, for I hardly know what it is that I do really suspect."

"O, I understand," said Claude; "you suspect that my father was badly treated, and had to leave France, and that this man was at the bottom of it. Well, I dare say he was, and that he is quite capable of any piece of villany; but as to his hunting us in America, I can acquit him of that charge, as far as my experience goes, for I never saw him, and never heard of any one ever being on our track. But can't you tell me something more definite about it? Can't you tell me exactly what you know?"

Mimi shook her head.

"I don't know anything," said she, "except what little I told you — that poor papa's trouble of mind comes from some wrong which he did to some Montresor, who had to go to America. And you may not be connected with that Montresor, after all; but I'm afraid you must be, and that — you — will have to be — poor papa's — enemy."

"Never!" said Claude, vehemently; "never! not if your father— Whatever has happened, I will let it pass — so far as I am concerned."

"O, you don't know what it is that has happened."

"Neither do you, for that matter; so there now; and for my part I don't want to know, and I won't try to find out, if you think I'd better not."

"I don't dare to think anything about it; I only know that a good son has duties towards his parents, and that he must devote his life to the vindication of their honor."

"Undoubtedly," said Claude, placidly; "but as it happens my parents have never communicated to me any story of any wrongs of theirs, I know very little about them. They never desired that I should investigate their lives; and, as I have never heard of any wrongs which they suffered, I don't see how I can go about to vindicate their honor. I have, by the merest chance, come upon something which excited my curiosity, and made me anxious to know something more. I have had no deeper feeling than curiosity; and if you think that my search will make me an enemy of your father, I hereby give up the search, and decline to pursue it any farther. In fact, I'll fall back upon my old name and rank, and become plain Claude Motier."

Claude tried to speak in an off-hand tone; but his assumed indifference could not conceal the deep devotion of the look which he gave to Mimi, or the profound emotion which was in his heart. It was for her sake that he thus offered to relinquish his purpose. She knew it and felt it.

"I'm sure," said she, "I don't know what to say to that. I'm afraid to say anything. I don't know what may happen yet; you may at any time find out something which would break through all your indifference, and fill you with a thirst for vengeance. I don't know, and you don't know, what may be — before us. So don't make any rash offers, but merely do as I asked you before; and that is, — while papa is here, — refrain from mentioning this subject to him. It is simply for the sake of his — his peace of mind — and — and — his health. I know it will excite him so dreadfully — that I tremble for the result."

"O, of course," said Claude, "I promise, as I did before. You needn't be at all afraid."

"Would you have any objection," she asked, after a short silence, "to tell me how much you do really know?"

"Of course not," said Claude, with his usual frankness. "I'll tell you the whole story. There isn't much of it. I always believed myself to be the son of Jean Motier, until a short time ago. We lived near Boston, a place that you, perhaps, have heard of. He was always careful to give me the best education that could be had in a colony, and particularly in all the accomplishments of a gentleman. We were both very happy, and lived very well, and I called him father, and he called me son; and so things went on until a few weeks ago. I went off hunting with some British officers, and on my return found the old man dying. The shock to me was a terrible one. At that time I believed that it was my father that I was losing. What made it worse, was the evident fact that there was something on his mind, something that he was longing to tell me; but he could not collect his thoughts, and he could only speak a few broken words.

He kept muttering, '*Mon trésor, Mon trésor;*' but I thought it was merely some loving words of endearment to me, and did not imagine what they really meant. Still I saw that there was something on his mind, and that he died without being able to tell it."

Claude paused for a moment, quite overcome by his recollections, and Mimi's large dark eyes filled with tears in her deep sympathy with his sorrows.

"Well," said Claude, regaining his composure with an effort, "I'll go on. As soon as he was buried I began to search the papers, partly to see how the business was, and how I was situated in the world; but more for the sake of trying to find out what this secret could be. There was an old cabinet filled with papers and parcels, and here I began my search. For a long time I found nothing but old business letters and receipts; but at last I found some religious books — with a name written in them. The name was Louise de Montresor. Well, no sooner had I seen this than I at once recollected the words of my father, as I supposed him, which I thought words of endearment — Montresor, Montresor. I saw now that it was the name of a person — of a woman; so this excited me greatly, and I continued the search with greater ardor.

"After a while I came to a drawer in which was a quantity of gold coins, amounting to over a hundred guineas. In this same drawer was a gold watch; on the back of it were engraved the letters L. D. M., showing that it was evidently the property of this Louise de Montresor. A gold chain was connected with it, upon which was fastened a seal. On this was engraved a griffin rampant, with the motto, *Noblesse oblige.*

"Well, after this I found another drawer, in which were several lady's ornaments, and among them was a package carefully wrapped up. On opening it I found the miniature portrait of a lady, and this lady was the same Louise de Montresor, for her name was written on the back."

"Have you it now?" asked Mimi, with intense interest.

"Yes," said Claude; "and I'll show it to you some time. But I have something else to show you just now. Wait a minute, and I'll explain. After I found the portrait, I went on searching, and came to another package. On opening this I found some papers which seemed totally different from anything I had seen as yet. The ink was faded; the writing was a plain, bold hand; and now I'll let you read this for yourself; and you'll know as much as I do."

Saying this, Claude produced from his pocket a paper, which he opened and handed to Mimi. It was a sheet of foolscap, written on three sides, in a plain, bold hand. The ink was quite faded. As Mimi took the paper, her hand trembled with excitement, and over her face there came a sudden anxious, half-frightened look, as though she dreaded to make herself acquainted with the contents of this old document.

After a moment's hesitation she mustered up her resolution, and began to read. It was as follows:—

"QUEBEC, June 10, 1725.

"Instructions to Jean Motier with reference to my son, Claude de Montresor, and my property.

"As I do not know how long I shall be absent, I think it better to leave directions about my son, which may be your guide in the event of my death. I must stay away long enough to enable me to overcome the grief that I feel. Long, long indeed, must it be before I shall feel able to settle in any one place. The death of my dearest wife, Louise, has left me desolate beyond expression, and there is no home for me any more on earth, since she has gone.

"I have property enough for you to bring up Claude as a gentleman. I wish him to have the best education which he can get in the colonies. I do not wish him to know about his family and the past history of his unhappy parents until he shall be old enough to judge for himself. In any case, I should wish him not to think of France. Let him content himself in America. It is done. In France there is no redress. The government is hopelessly corrupt, and there is no possibility of wrong being righted. Besides, the laws against the Huguenots are in full force, and he can never live with his mother's enemies. I revere the sacred memory of my Huguenot wife, and curse the knaves and fanatics who wronged her and cast her out; yet I thank God that I was able to save her from the horrible fate that awaited her.

"I wish my son, therefore, to know nothing of France, at least until he shall be of age, and his own master; and even then I should wish him never to go there. Let him content himself in the colonies. For how could he ever redeem the position which is lost? or how could he hope to face the powerful and unscrupulous enemies who have wrought my ruin; the false friend who betrayed me; his base and infernal accomplice; the ungrateful government which did such foul wrong to a loyal servant? All is lost. The estates are confiscated. The unjust deed can never be undone. Let my son, therefore, resign himself to fate, and be content with the position in which he may find himself.

"The property will be sufficient to maintain him in comfort and independence. Here he will have all that he may want; here the church will give him her consolations without bigotry, or fanaticism, or corruption, or persecution. He will be free from the vices and temptations of the old world, and will have a happier fate than that of his unhappy father.

"EUGENE DE MONTRESOR."

Another paper was folded up with this. It was written in a different hand, and was as follows: —

"BOSTON, June 20, 1740.

"Count Eugene de Montresor left on the 2d July, 1725, and has never since been heard of. I have followed all his instructions, with one exception. It was from the countess that I first heard the word of life, and learned the truth. The priests at Quebec gave me no peace; and so I had to leave and come here, among a people who are of another nation, but own and hold my faith — the faith of the pure worship of Christ. The count wished me to bring you up a Catholic; but I had a higher duty than his will, and I have brought you up not in your father's religion, but in your mother's faith. Your father was a good man, though in error. He has, no doubt, long since rejoined the saint who was his wife on earth; and I know that the spirits of your father and mother smile approvingly on my acts.

"If I die before I tell you all, dear Claude, you will see this, and will understand that I did my duty to your parents and to you—"

Here it ended abruptly. There was no name, and it was evidently unfinished.

CHAPTER VI.

A FRENCH FRIGATE.

MIMI read both papers through rapidly and breathlessly, and having finished them, she read them over once more. As she finished the second reading, Claude presented to her in silence a small package. She took it in the same silence. On opening it, she saw inside a miniature portrait of a lady — the same one which Claude had mentioned. She was young and exquisitely beautiful, with rich dark hair, that flowed luxuriantly around her head; soft hazel eyes, that rested with inexpressible sweetness upon the spectator; and a gentle, winning smile. This face produced an unwonted impression upon Mimi. Long and eagerly did she gaze upon it, and when, at length, she handed it back to Claude, her eyes were moist with tears.

Claude replaced the portrait in its wrapper, and then restored it, with the letters, to his pocket. For some time they sat in silence, and then Claude said, —

"You see there is no great duty laid on me. Judging by the tone of that letter, I should be doing my duty to my father if I did not go to France — and if I did not seek after anything."

"Ah! but how could you possibly live, and leave all this unexplained?"

"I could do it very easily," said Claude.

"You don't know yourself."

"O, yes, I could; I could live very easily and very happily — if I only had your assistance."

At these words, which were spoken in a low, earnest voice, full of hidden meaning, Mimi darted a rapid glance at Claude, and caught his eyes fixed on her. Her own eyes fell before the fervid eagerness of the young man's gaze, a flush overspread her face, and she said not a word. Nor did Claude say anything more just then; but it was rather as though he felt afraid of having gone too far, for he instantly changed the subject.

"I'm afraid," said he, "that I shall not be able to find out very much. You cannot give me any enlightenment, and there is nothing very precise in these papers. The chief thing that I learned from them was the fact that Jean Motier was not my father, but my guardian. Then a few other things are stated which can easily be mentioned. First, that my father was the Count Eugene de Montresor; then that he was driven to exile by some false charge which he did not seem able to meet; then, that his estates were confiscated; then, that his wife, my mother, was a Huguenot, and also in danger. I see, also, that my father considered his enemies altogether too powerful for any hope to remain that he could resist them, and that finally, after my mother's death, he grew weary of the world, and went away somewhere to die.

"Now, the fact that he lived two years in Quebec made me have some thoughts at first of going there; but afterwards I recollected how long it had been since he was there, and it seemed quite improbable that I should find any one now who could tell me anything about him; while, if I went to France, I thought it might be comparatively easy to learn the cause of his exile and punishment. And so, as I couldn't find any vessels going direct from Boston, I concluded to go to Louisbourg and take ship there. I thought also that I might find out something at Louisbourg; though what I expected I can hardly say.

"You spoke as though you supposed that this Cazeneau had something to do with my father's trouble. Do you think that his present journey has anything to do with it? That is, do you think he is coming out on the same errand as your father?"

"I really do not know what to say about that. I should think not. I know that he has some office in Louisbourg, and I do not see what motive he can have to search after the Montresors. I believe that papa hopes to find your papa, so as to make some atonement, or something of that sort; but I do not believe that Cazeneau is capable of making atonement for anything. I do not believe that Cazeneau has a single good quality. Cazeneau is my father's evil genius."

Mimi spoke these words with much vehemence, not caring, in her excitement, whether she was overheard or not; but scarce had she uttered them than she saw emerging from the forecastle the head of Cazeneau himself. She stopped short, and looked at him in amazement and consternation. He bowed blandly, and coming upon deck, walked past her to the stern. After he had passed, Mimi looked at Claude with a face full of vexation.

"Who could have supposed," said she, "that he was so near? He must have heard every word!"

"Undoubtedly he did," said Claude, "and he had a chance of verifying the old adage that 'listeners never hear good of themselves.'"

"O, I wish you would be on your guard!" said Mimi, in real distress. "It makes me feel very anxious."

She threw at Claude a glance so full of tender interest and pathetic appeal, that Claude's playful mood gave way to one of a more sentimental character; and it is quite impossible to tell what he would have done or said had not Cazeneau again made his appearance, on his way back to the forecastle.

He smiled a cold smile as he passed them.

"Charming weather for a *tête-à-tête*, mademoiselle," said he. "*Parbleu!* Monsieur Motier, I don't wonder you don't make your vessel go faster. I quite envy you; but at present I must see about my fellows below here."

With these words he turned away, and descended into the forecastle. Mimi also turned away, and Claude accompanied her to the stern.

"How old do you suppose he is?" asked Claude, very gravely.

"How old? What a funny question! Why, he must be nearly fifty by this time."

"Fifty!" exclaimed Claude, in surprise.

"Yes."

"Why, I thought he was about thirty, or thirty-five."

"Well, he certainly doesn't look over forty; but he is a wonderfully well-kept man. Even on the raft, the ruling passion remained strong in the very presence of death, and he managed to keep up his youthful appearance; but I know that he is almost, if not quite, as old as papa."

"Is it possible?" cried Claude, in amazement.

Mimi turned, and with her face close to Claude's, regarded him with an anxious look, and spoke in a low, hurried voice:—

"O, be on your guard — beware of him. Even now he is engaged in some plot against you. I know it by his face. That's what takes him down there to confer with the seamen. He is not to be trusted. He is all false — in face, in figure, in mind, and in heart. He knows nothing about honor, or justice, or mercy. He has been the deadly enemy of the Montresors, and if he finds out who you are, he will be your deadly enemy. O, don't smile that way! Don't despise this enemy! Be careful — be on your guard, I entreat you —*for my sake!*"

These last words were spoken in a hurried whisper, and the next moment Mimi turned and hastened down into the cabin to her father, while Claude remained there, thinking over these words. Yet of them all it was not the warning contained in them that was present in his memory, but rather the sweet meaning conveyed in those last three words, and in the tone in which they were uttered — the words *for my sake!*

Out of his meditations on this theme he was at length aroused by an exclamation from Zac. Looking up, he saw that worthy close beside him, intently watching something far away on the horizon, through a glass.

"I'll be darned if it ain't a French frigate!"

This was the exclamation that roused Claude. He at once returned to himself, and turning to Zac, he asked him what he meant. Zac said nothing, but, handing him the spy-glass, pointed away to the west, where a sail was visible on the horizon. That sail was an object of curious interest to others on board; to the lieutenant and seamen of the wrecked vessel, who were staring at her from the bows; and to Cazeneau, who was with them, staring with equal interest. Claude took the glass, and raising it to his eye, examined the strange sail long and carefully, but without being able to distinguish anything in particular about her.

"What makes you think that she is a French frigate?" he asked, as he handed the glass back to Zac. "I cannot make out that she is French any more than English."

"O, I can tell easy enough," said Zac, "by the cut of her jib. Then, too, I judge by her course. That there craft is comin' down out of the Bay of Fundy, which the Moosoos in their lingo call Fonde de la Baie. She's been up at some of the French settlements. Now, she may be goin' to France — or mayhap she's goin' to Louisbourg — an' if so be as she's goin' to Louisbourg, why, I shouldn't wonder if it mightn't be a good idea for our French friends here to go aboard of her and finish their voyage in a vessel of their own. One reason why I'd rather have it so is, that I don't altogether like the manœuvrin's of that French count over thar. He's too sly; an' he's up to somethin', an' I don't fancy havin' to keep up a eternal watch agin him. If I was well red of him I could breathe freer; but at the same time I don't altogether relish the idee of puttin' myself into the clutches of that thar frigate. It's easy enough for me to keep out of her way; but if I was once to get under her guns, thar'd be an end of the Parson. This here count ain't to be trusted, no how; an' if he once got into communication with that there frigate, he'd be my master. An' so I'm in a reg'lar quan-dary, an' no mistake. Darned if I know what in the blamenation to do about it."

Zac stopped short, and looked with an air of mild inquiry at Claude. Claude, on his part, was rather startled by Zac's estimate of the character of Cazeneau, for it chimed in so perfectly with Mimi's opinion that it affected him in spite of himself. But it was only for a moment, and then his own self-confidence gained the mastery.

CHAPTER VII.

CAUGHT IN A TRAP.

THE schooner was now directed towards the stranger, and before very long they saw that her course had been changed, and that she was now bearing down upon them. Zac stood at the helm saying nothing, but keeping his eyes fixed upon the frigate, which drew nearer and nearer, till finally she came near enough for her flag to be plainly seen. They had been right in their conjectures, and the new comer was a French frigate. This assurance seemed to open the mouth of Zac.

"I must say," he remarked to Claude, "the nearer I get to her, the less I like it. I've met Moosoo before this on the high seas, but I allus went on the plan of keepin' out of his way. This here system of goin' right into his jaws don't suit me at all."

"O, come now," said Claude, "don't begin again. I thought you'd given up all anxiety. There's not the slightest occasion for being worried about it. I'll find out whether they can take me to Louisbourg, and if so I'll leave you, and you'll get back to Boston quicker than if you took me where you first proposed."

"Yes; but suppose she's goin' to France, and chooses to take me prisoner?" said Zac.

"O, nonsense!" said Claude. "They couldn't. What, after saving so many lives, and conveying these rescued fellow-countrymen to their own flag, do you suppose they could think of arresting you? Nonsense! The thing's impossible."

Zac said no more, but was evidently ill at ease, and in his own mind there was no end of dark forebodings as to the event of this meeting. These forebodings were in no way lessened as the schooner rounded to under the lee of the frigate, and Zac saw a row of guns heavy enough to blow him and his "Parson" to atoms. The frigate did not wait for the schooner to send a boat aboard, for her own boat was all ready, and soon appeared, well manned, rowing towards the schooner. On coming alongside, the officer in command stepped on board, and Claude at once went forward to meet him. Cazeneau also walked forward with the same purpose.

Claude politely raised his hat, and the officer civilly returned his greeting.

"This, monsieur, is the schooner Amos Adams, of Boston. We have recently picked up the survivors of His Royal French Majesty's frigate 'Arethuse,' which has been lost at sea, and we have come to see whether you could take them. Will you have the goodness to tell me where you are going?"

"Mon Dieu!" exclaimed the officer, "the Arethuse lost! Is it possible? What a terrible misfortune! And she had on board the new commandant for Louisbourg."

At this Cazeneau came forward.

"He is safe, monsieur, for I am he."

The officer respectfully removed his hat, and bowed very low.

"What ship is this?" asked Cazeneau, in the tone of a superior.

"L'Aigle," replied the officer.

"Where are you bound?"

"To Brest. We have just been cruising to the different settlements and forts on the Bay of Fundy, with some supplies which were sent from Louisbourg."

"Ah! And you are now on your return to France?"

"Yes."

"Who commands your ship?"

"Captain Ducrot."

"Ah! Very good. You see, monsieur," said Cazeneau to Claude, "this ship is bound to France; and that destination will not suit any of us. I think I had better go aboard and see the captain, with whom I may have some little influence. Perhaps, as my command is an important one, he may be persuaded to alter his course, and land us at Louisbourg, or some other place. — And so, monsieur," he continued, turning to the officer, "I shall be obliged to you if you will put me aboard the Aigle."

The officer assured him that the boat was altogether at his service; whereupon Cazeneau stepped aboard, followed by the officer, and in a short time the boat was on its way back to the frigate. Claude watched this in silence, and without any misgivings. It seemed to him quite natural, and, indeed, the best thing that could be done, under the circumstances. If the ship was going to France, she could not be of service to them; but if her captain could be induced to change his course and land them at Louisbourg, this would be exactly what they wanted; and Cazeneau seemed to be the only one on board who was at all likely to persuade the captain of the Aigle to do such a thing as this.

It seemed a long time before any further notice was taken of the schooner. Meanwhile, all on board were watching the frigate with much anxiety, and wondering what the result would be. In any case it did not seem a matter of very great importance to any one; for the lieutenant and the two sailors, who might have been most concerned, were very well treated on board the schooner, — better, perhaps, than they would be on board a frigate, — and evinced no particular desire to leave. The priest said nothing; and to him, as well as to Claude, there was nothing to be gained by taking to the ship. As for the aged Laborde, he was still too weak to take any notice of events going on around him; while Mimi, perhaps, found herself as well situated here, under the care of Claude, as she could possibly be on the larger ship, under the care of one who might be less agreeable. Claude himself would certainly have preferred letting things remain as they were. The situation was very pleasant. Mimi's occasional companionship seemed sweeter than anything he had ever known; and, as he was master on board, he naturally had a certain right to show her attentions; which right he could not have under other circumstances. He would have liked to see Cazeneau take his departure for good, together with the French sailors, leaving Laborde and Mimi on board the schooner. Finally, Zac was not at all pleased with anything in his present situation. The thought of possible foul play never left his mind for an instant; and though the blow was delayed for a considerable time, he could not help feeling sure that it would fall.

During this period of waiting, the aged Laborde

had been brought up on deck, and placed there on a seat. This was done from a hope which Mimi had that he would be benefited by the excitement of the change. The sight of the ship, however, produced but little effect of any kind upon the languid and worn-out old man. He gave an indifferent glance at the frigate and the surrounding scene, and then subsided into himself, while Mimi in vain strove to rouse him from his indifference.

At last their suspense came to an end, and they saw preparations making for another visit to the schooner. This time a second boat was lowered, which was filled with marines. The sight of this formidable boat's crew produced on Claude an impression of surprise; while in Zac it enforced a conviction that his worst fears were now to be realized.

"Look thar!" said he in a hoarse whisper. "Now you see what's a comin'! Good by, poor old Parson! Yer in the claws of the Philistines now, an' no mistake."

To this Claude made no reply, for he began to feel rather perplexed himself, and to imagine that Cazeneau might have been playing him false. All that Mimi had said about him now came to his mind, and the armed boat's crew seemed like the first act of a traitor. He tried to account for this in some other way, but was not able. He could no longer laugh away Zac's fears. He could only be still and wait.

The two boats rowed towards the schooner. Cazeneau was not in either of them. He had remained on board. At length one of the boats touched the schooner, and the same officer who had visited her before again stepped on board.

"Is the Count de Laborde here?" he asked.

Claude pointed to where the old man was seated. The officer advanced, and removed his hat with a bow to the old count, and another to the beautiful Mimi.

"Monsieur le Comte," said he, "I have the honor to convey to you the compliments of Captain Ducrot, with the request that you would honor him with your company on board the Aigle. His excellency the Comte de Cazeneau, commandant of Louisbourg, has persuaded him to convey himself, and you, and some others, to the nearest French fort. It is the intention of Captain Ducrot to sail back up the Bay of Fundy, and land you at Grand Pré, from which place you can reach Louisbourg by land."

To this Laborde murmured a few indistinct words in reply, while Mimi made no remark whatever. She was anxious to know what Claude was intending to do. The officer now turned away to the others.

"My instructions," said he, "are, to convey the invitation of Captain Ducrot to Monsieur l'Abbé Michel and Lieutenant d'Angers, whom he will be happy to receive on board the Aigle, and convey them to Grand Pré, or France. The two seamen of the Arethuse will also go on board and report themselves."

The officer now went back to Laborde, and offered to assist him. The old man rose, and taking his arm, walked feebly towards the vessel's side, whence he descended into the boat, and was assisted to the stern by the seamen. The officer then assisted Mimi to a place by her father's side, anticipating Claude, who stepped forward with the offer of his assistance. Then followed Père Michel, and Lieutenant d'Angers, of the Arethuse; then Margot; and, finally, the two seamen.

Meanwhile nothing was said to Claude. He was not included in the compliments of Captain Ducrot, nor was any notice taken of him in any way. He could not help feeling slighted and irritated at the whole proceeding. To himself and to Zac this whole party owed their lives, and they were all leaving him now with no more regard for him than if he were a perfect stranger. But the fact was, the whole party took it for granted that he and Zac would be invited on board, and that they would see them both again, and supposed that they were coming in the same boat. Mimi and Père Michel both thought that Claude, at least, was going with them; for he had told them both that he was going to leave the schooner and send Zac home.

But Claude's feelings were somewhat embittered by this whole incident, and were destined to be still more so before it was all over.

The lieutenant remained on board. The boat rowed back to the Aigle, carrying the passengers above named, after which the lieutenant motioned to the other boat. This one moved alongside, and a half-dozen armed seamen stepped on board.

"Monsieur," said the lieutenant, advancing to Claude, "I hope you will pardon me for being the instrument in a very unpleasant duty. I am pained to inform you that you are my prisoner, on the command of his excellency the commandant of Louisbourg, whose instructions I am ordered to fulfil. I deeply regret this painful necessity, and most sincerely hope that it may prove only a temporary inconvenience."

At this Claude was so astounded that for some time he could only stare at the officer, without being able to utter a syllable. At length he said,—

"What, monsieur! A prisoner? You must be mistaken! And who— The commandant of Louisbourg — is not that the Count de Cazeneau?"

"It is."

"But, monsieur, it must be a mistake. I have never injured him or any one. I have done nothing but good to him. My friend here, the captain of this schooner, and I, saved his life; and we have treated him with the utmost kindness since he was on board here. Finally, we sailed towards you, and put ourselves in your power, solely that these shipwrecked passengers, of whom the Count de Cazeneau was one, might reach their friends sooner. How, then, can he possibly mean to arrest me?"

"Monsieur, I assure you that it grieves me most deeply," said the officer — "most exquisitely. I know all this — all, and so does Captain Ducrot; but there is no mistake, and it must be."

"But what authority has he here, and why should your captain do his orders?"

"Monsieur, I am only a subordinate, and I know nothing but my orders. At the same time, you must know that the commandant of Louisbourg has general control, by land and sea, and is my captain's superior."

Claude made no reply. He saw that this man was but, as he said, a subordinate, and was only obeying his orders. But the officer had something still on his mind. His words and his looks all showed that the present business was exceedingly distasteful to him, and that he was only doing it under pressure.

"Monsieur," said he, after a pause, "I have another painful duty to perform. I am ordered to take possession of this schooner, as a prize of war, and take the captain and crew as prisoners of war."

At this Claude stared at the officer once more. utterly stupefied.

"Mon Dieu!" he cried, at length. "Are you a Frenchman? Is your captain a French gentleman? Do you know, monsieur, what you are doing? We have saved some shipwrecked Frenchmen; we have carried them to a place of safety; and for this we are arrested! This honest man, the captain, might expect a reward for his generosity; and what does he get? Why, he is seized as a prisoner of war, and his schooner is made a prize! Is there any chivalry left in France? Are these the acts of Frenchmen? Great Heavens! Has it come to this?"

"Monsieur," said the officer, "be calm, I implore you. All this gives me the most exquisite distress. But I must obey orders."

"You are right," said Claude. "You are a subordinate. I am wasting words to talk with you. Take me to your captain, or to the Count de Cazeneau. Let me learn what it is that induces him to act towards us with such unparalleled baseness."

"Monsieur, I shall be happy to do all that I can. I will take you to the Aigle,— under guard,— and you will be a prisoner there. I hope that his excellency will accord you the favor of an interview."

All this time Zac had been a silent spectator of the scene. He had not understood the words that were spoken, but he had gathered the general meaning of this scene from the gestures and expression of the two speakers. The presence, also, of the armed guard was enough to show him that the blow which he dreaded had fallen. And now, since the worst had happened, all his uneasiness departed, and he resumed all the vigor of his mind. He at once decided upon the best course to follow, and that course was to be emphatically one of quiet, and calmness, and cool watchfulness. Claude had become excited at this event; Zac had become cool.

"Wal," said he, advancing towards Claude, "it's just as I said. I allus said that these here frog-eatin' Frenchmen wan't to be trusted; and here, you see, I was right. I see about how it is. The poor, unfort'nate Parson's done for, an' I'm in for it, too, I s'pose."

Claude turned, and gave Zac a look of indescribable distress.

"There's some infernal villain at work, Zac," said he, "out of the common course, altogether. I'm arrested myself."

"You? Ah!" said Zac, who did not appear to be at all surprised. "You don't say so! Wal, you've got the advantage of me, since you can speak their darned lingo. So they've gone an' 'rested you, too — have they?"

"It's that infernal Cazeneau," said Claude; "and I haven't got the faintest idea why."

"Cazeneau, is it? O, well," said Zac, "they're all alike. It's my opinion that it's the captain of the frigate, an' he's doin' it in Cazeneau's name. Ye see he's ben a cruisin' about, an' hankers after a prize; an' I'm the only one he's picked up. You're 'rested — course — as one of the belongin's of the Parson. You an' I an' the hull crew: that's it! We're all prisoners of war!"

"O, no," said Claude. "It isn't that, altogether; there's some deeper game."

"Pooh!" said Zac; "the game ain't a deep one, at all; it's an every-day game. But I must say it is hard to be done for jest because we had a leetle too much hooman feelin'. Now, ef we'd only let them Frenchies rot and drown on their raft, — or ef we'd a' taken them as prisoners to Boston, — we'd ben spared this present tribulation."

Zac heaved a sigh as he said this, and turned away. Then a sudden thought struck him.

"O, look here," said he; "jest ask 'em one thing, as a partiklar favor. You needn't mention me, though. It's this. Ask 'em if they won't leave me free — that is, I don't want to be handcuffed."

"Handcuffed!" exclaimed Claude, grinding his teeth in futile rage. "They won't dare to do that!"

"O, you jest ask this Moosoo, as a favor. They needn't object."

Upon this Claude turned to the officer.

"Monsieur," said he, "I have a favor to ask. I and my friend here are your prisoners, but we do not wish to be treated with unnecessary indignity or insult. I ask, then, that we may be spared the insult of being bound. Our offence has not been great. We have only saved the lives of six of your fellow-countrymen. Is it presumption to expect this favor?"

"Monsieur," said the officer, "I assure you that, as far as I have anything to say, you shall not be bound. And as to this brave fellow, he may be at liberty to move about in this schooner as long as he is quiet and gives no offence — that is, for the present. And now, monsieur, I will ask you to accompany me on board the Aigle."

With these words the officer prepared to quit the schooner. Before doing so he addressed some words to the six seamen, who were to be left in charge as a prize crew, with one midshipman at their head. He directed them to follow the frigate until further orders, and also, until further orders, to leave the captain of the schooner unbound, and let him have the run of the vessel.

After this the officer returned to the Aigle, taking Claude with him.

CHAPTER VIII.

UNDER ARREST.

BY the time that Claude reached the Aigle, the evening of this eventful day was at hand. He was taken to a room on the gun-deck, which seemed as though used for a prison, from the general character of the bolts and bars, and other fixtures. Claude asked to see the captain, and the lieutenant promised to carry the message to him. After about an hour he came back with the message that the captain could not see him that evening. Upon this Claude begged him to ask Count de Cazeneau for an interview. The officer went off once more, and returned with the same answer. Upon this Claude was compelled to submit to his fate as best he might. It was a hard thing for him, in the midst of health, and strength, and joy, with all the bounding activity and eager energy of youth, to be cast down into a prison; but to be arrested and imprisoned under such circumstances; to be so foully wronged by the very man whose life he had saved; to have his own kindness and hospitality repaid by treachery, and bonds, and insult, — all this was galling in the highest degree, and well nigh intolerable.

That night Claude did not sleep. He lay awake wondering what could be the cause of Cazeneau's enmity, and trying in vain to conjecture.

All the next morning Claude waited for some message from Captain Ducrot; but none came. His breakfast was brought to him, consisting of the coarse fare of common seamen, and then his dinner; but the captain did not make his appearance. Even the officer who had arrested him, and who had hitherto shown himself sufficiently sympathetic, did not appear. The sailor who brought his meals gave no answer to his questions. It seemed to Claude as though his captors were unwilling to give him a hearing.

At length, in about the middle of the afternoon, Claude heard the tramp of men approaching his prison; the door was opened, and he saw an officer enter, while three marines, with fixed bayonets, stood outside.

"Have I the honor of speaking to Captain Ducrot?" asked Claude.

"I am Captain Ducrot," said the other.

He was a small, wiry man, dressed with extreme neatness, who looked rather like an attorney than a seaman. His voice was thin and harsh; his manner cold and repulsive, with an air of primness and formality that made him seem more like a machine than a man. The first sight of him made Claude feel as though any appeal to his humanity or generosity, or even justice, would be useless. He looked like an automaton, fit to obey the will of another, but without any independent will of his own. Nevertheless, Claude had no other resource; so he began : —

"I have asked for this interview, monsieur," said he, "from a conviction that there must be some mistake. Listen to me for a moment. I have lived in Boston all my life. I was on my way to Louisbourg, intending to go to France from there, on business. I had engaged a schooner to take me to Louisbourg; and at sea I came across a portion of the wreck of the Arethuse, with six people on board, one of whom was the Count de Cazeneau. I saved them all — that is, with the assistance of the captain of the schooner. After I brought them on board the schooner, I treated them all with the utmost kindness; and finally, when I saw your ship in the distance, I voluntarily sailed towards you, for the purpose of allowing my passengers to go on board. I had designed coming on board myself also, if your your destination suited my views. And now, monsieur, for all this I find myself arrested, held here in prison, treated as a common felon, and all because I have saved the lives of some shipwrecked fellow-beings. Monsieur, it is not possible that this can be done with your knowledge. If you want confirmation of my words, ask the good priest Père Michel, and he will confirm all that I have said."

The captain listened to all this very patiently, and without any interruption. At length, as Claude ended, he replied, —

"But you yourself cannot suppose that you, as you say, are imprisoned merely for this. People do not arrest their benefactors merely because they are their benefactors; and if you have saved the life of his excellency, you cannot suppose that he has ordered your arrest for that sole reason. Monsieur has more good sense, and must understand well that there is some sort of charge against him."

"Monsieur," said Claude, "I swear to you I not only know no reason for my arrest, but I cannot even imagine one; and I entreat you, as a man of honor, to tell me what the charge against me is."

"Monsieur," said the captain, blandly, "we are both men of honor, of course. Of your honor I have no doubt. It is untouched. Every day men of honor, and of rank, too, are getting into difficulties; and whenever one meddles with political affairs it must be so."

"Political affairs!" cried Claude. "What have I to do with political affairs?"

The captain again smiled blandly.

"*Parbleu*, monsieur, but that is not for me to say."

"But is that the charge against me?"

"Most certainly. How could it be otherwise?"

"Politics, politics!" cried Claude. "I don't understand you! I must be taken for some other person."

"O, no," said the captain; "there's no mistake."

"Pardon me, monsieur, there must be."

"Then, monsieur, allow me to indulge the hope that you may be able to show where the mistake is, at your trial."

The captain made a movement now as though he was about to leave; but Claude detained him.

"One moment, monsieur," said he. "Will you not tell me something more? Will you not tell me what these political charges are? For, I swear to you, I cannot imagine. How can I, who have lived all my life in Boston, be connected with politics in any way? Let me know, then, something about these charges; for nothing is more distressing than to be in a situation like this, and have no idea whatever of the cause of it."

"*Eh bien*, monsieur," said the captain, "since you

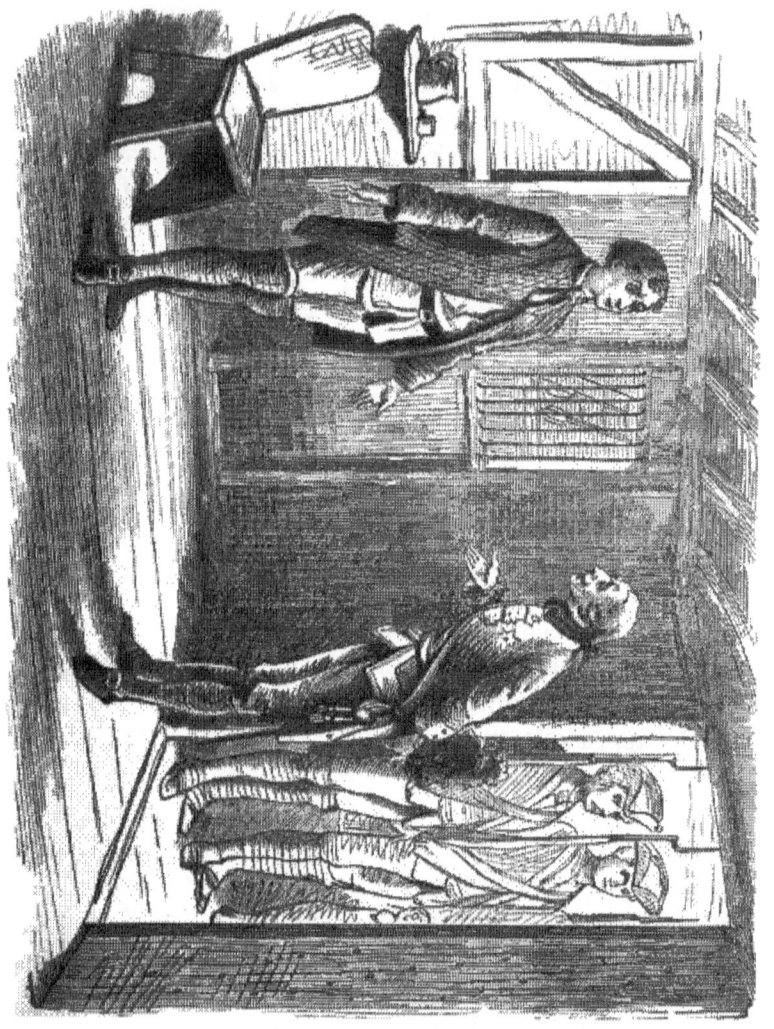

"Of your Honor I have no Doubt." Page 88.

wish it, I have no objection whatever to state what they are; and if you can clear yourself and show your innocence, I shall be the first to congratulate you. His excellency will not object to my telling you, I am sure, for he is the soul of goodness, and is full of generous impulses. Very well, then. In the first place you call yourself Claude Motier. Now, this is said to be an assumed name. Your real name is said to be Claude de Montresor; and it is said that you are the son of a certain Eugene de Montresor, who committed grave offences about twenty years ago, for which he would have been severely punished had he not fled from the country. His wife, also, — your mother, perhaps, — was proscribed, and would have been arrested and punished had she not escaped with her husband. They were then outlawed, and their estates were confiscated. The wife died, the husband disappeared. This is what happened to them."

"That is all true," said Claude. "But my father and mother were both most foully wronged — "

"Pardon, monsieur," said the captain. "That is very probable; but I am not here as judge; I am only giving you information about the charge against you. I have not time to listen to your answer; and I would advise you not to speak too hastily. You have already confessed to the assumed name. I would advise you to be careful in your statements. And now, monsieur, should you like to hear any more?"

"Yes, yes!" cried Claude, eagerly; "tell me all that there is to know."

"Very well," said the captain. "Now you, under an assumed name, engage a schooner to take you, not to Louisbourg, but to some place in the vicinity of Louisbourg. Being the son of two dangerous political offenders, who were both outlawed for grave crimes, you are found coming from Boston to Louisbourg under an assumed name, and upon a secret errand, which you keep to yourself. Under these circumstances the commandant could not overlook your case. It seemed to him one which was full of suspicion, and, in spite of the gratitude which he felt for your kind offices, he nevertheless was compelled, by a strong sense of public duty, to order your arrest. You will be accorded a fair trial; and, though appearances are against you, you may succeed in proving your innocence; in which case, monsieur, I am sure that no one will be more rejoiced than myself and his excellency.

" You have also complained, monsieur, of the arrest of your captain. That was done on account of his unfortunate connection with you. He may be innocent, but that remains to be seen. At present appearances are against him, and he must take his share of the guilt which attaches to you. His arrest was a political necessity."

After this the captain left; and, as Claude saw how useless it was to attempt to plead his cause to this man, he made no further attempt to detain him.

Left once more to his own reflections, Claude recalled all that the captain had said, and at first was lost in wonder at the gravity of the charges that had been raised up against him. Nor could he conceal from himself that, though they were based on nothing, they still were serious and formidable. Even in France charges of a political kind would lead to serious consequences; and here in the colonies he felt less sure of justice. Indeed, as far as justice was concerned, he hardly hoped to experience anything of the kind, for his judge would be the very man who had got up these charges, and had treated him with such baseness and treachery. The fact was, that he would be called before a court where accuser, witness, and judge would all be one and the same person, and, what was more, the person who for some reason had chosen to become his bitterest enemy. Dark indeed and gloomy was the prospect that now lowered before him.

Before an impartial court the charges against him might be answered or refuted; but where could he find such a court? Cazeneau had created the charges, and would know how to make them still more formidable. And now he felt that behind these charges there must lurk something more dangerous still.

Already there had arisen in his mind certain suspicions as to Cazeneau's designs upon Mimi. These suspicions he had hinted at in conversation with her, and his present circumstances deepened them into convictions. It began now to seem to him that Cazeneau had designs to make the beautiful, high-born girl his wife. Everything favored him. He was supreme in authority out here; the old Laborde was under his influence; the daughter's consent alone was wanting. Of that consent, under ordinary circumstances, he could make sure. But he had seen a close and strong friendship arising between Mimi and her preserver. This Claude considered as a better and more probable cause for his hate. If this were indeed so, and if this hate grew up out of jealousy, then his prospects were indeed dark, for jealousy is as cruel as the grave.

The more Claude thought of this, the greater was the importance which he attached to it. It seemed to be this which had made Cazeneau transform himself into an eavesdropper; this which had occasioned his dark looks, his morose words, and haughty reticence. In his eavesdropping he must have heard enough to excite his utmost jealousy; and Claude, in recalling his conversations with Mimi, could remember words which must have been gall and bitterness to such a jealous listener.

CHAPTER IX.

GRAND PRE.

NEARLY thirty years before this, the French government had been compelled to give up the possession of Acadie to the English, and to retire to the Island of Cape Breton. Here they had built a stronghold at Louisbourg, which they were enlarging and strengthening every year, to the great disgust and alarm of the New England colonies. But though Acadie had been given up to the English, it could hardly be said to be held by them. Only two posts were occupied, the one at Canso, in the strait that separated Cape Breton from Acadie, and the other at Annapolis Royal. At Canso there was a wooden block-house, with a handful of soldiers; while at Annapolis Royal, where the English governor resided, the fortifications were more extensive, yet in a miserable condition. At this last place there were a few companies of soldiers, and here the governor tried to perform the difficult task of transforming the French Acadians to loyal British subjects.

But the French at Louisbourg never forgot their fellow-countrymen, and never relinquished their designs on Acadie. The French inhabitants of that province amounted to several thousands, who occupied the best portions of the country, while the English consisted of only a few individuals in one or two posts. Among the French Acadians emissaries were constantly moving about, who sought to keep up among them their old loyalty to the French crown, and by their pertinacity sorely disturbed the peace of the English governor at Annapolis Royal. The French governor at Louisbourg was not slow to second these efforts by keeping the Acadians supplied with arms and ammunition; and it was for this purpose that the Aigle had been sent to the settlements up the Bay of Fundy.

Up the bays he now sailed, in accordance with the wish of Cazeneau. His reason for this course was, that he might see the people for himself, and judge how far they might be relied on in the event of war, which he knew must soon be declared. It was his intention to land at Grand Pré, the chief Acadian settlement, and thence proceed by land to Louisbourg. He had understood from Captain Ducrot that an Indian trail went all the way through the woods, which could be traversed on horseback. Such a course would impose more hardship upon the aged Laborde and Mimi than would be encountered on shipboard; but Cazeneau had his own purposes, which were favored, to a great extent, by the land route. Besides, he had the schooner with him, so that if, after all, it should be advisable to go by water, they could make the journey in her.

The Aigle sailed, and the schooner followed. The wind had changed, and now blew more steadily, and from a favorable quarter. The currents delayed them somewhat; but on the third morning after the two vessels had met, they reached the entrance of the Basin of Minas.

The scenery here was wild and grand. A few miles from the shore there rose a lofty rocky island, precipitous on all sides save one, its summit crested with trees, its base worn by the restless waves. Opposite this was a rocky shore, with cliffs crowned with the primeval forest. From this pond the strait began, and went on for miles, till it reached the Basin, forming a majestic avenue, with a sublime gateway. On one side of this gateway were rocky shores receding into wooded hills, while on the other was a towering cliff standing apart from the shore, rising abruptly from the water, torn by the tempest and worn by the tide. From this the precipitous cliff ran on for miles, forming one side of the strait, till it terminated in a majestic promontory.

This promontory rose on one side, and on the other a lofty, wooded island, inside of which was a winding shore, curving into a harbor. Here the strait terminated, and beyond this the waters of the Basin of Minas spread away for many a mile, surrounded on every side by green, wooded shores. In one place was a cluster of small islands; in another, rivers rolled their turbid floods, bearing with them the sediment of long and fertile valleys. The blue waters sparkled in the sun under the blue sky; the sea-gulls whirled and screamed through the air; nowhere could the eye discern any of the works of man. It seemed like some secluded corner of the universe, and as if those on board the ship

> "were the first that ever burst
> Into that silent sea."

But, though not visible from this point, the settlements of man were here, and the works of human industry lying far away on the slopes of distant hills and the edges of low, marshy shores.

It was not without much caution that they had passed through the strait. They had waited for the tide to come in, and then, with a favorable wind, they had made the venture. Borne onward by wind and tide together, they sailed on far into the bay, and then, directing their course to the southward, they sailed onward for a few miles farther. The captain had been here before, and was anxious to find his former anchorage. On the former occasion he had waited outside and sent in for a pilot, but now he had ventured inside without one, trusting to his memory. He knew well the perils that attend upon navigation in this place, and was not inclined to risk too much. For here were the highest tides in the world to be encountered, and swift currents, and sudden gusts of wind, and far-spreading shoals and treacherous quicksands, among which the unwary navigator could come to destruction only too easily.

But no accident happened on this occasion; the navigation was made with the utmost circumspection, the schooner being sent ahead to sound all the way, and the ship following. At length both came to anchor at a distance from the shore of about five miles. Nearer than that the captain did not dare to go, for fear of the sand-banks and shoals.

Here a boat was lowered, and Cazeneau prepared to land, together with the aged Laborde and Mimi. The Abbé Michel also prepared to accompany them.

Ever since Laborde had been saved from the wreck, he had been weak and listless. It seemed as though the exhaustion, and exposure, and privation of that event had utterly broken down his constitution. Since he had been taken to the ship, however, he had grown much worse, and was no longer able to walk. He had not risen from his berth since he had come on board the Aigle. Mimi's anxiety about him had been excessive, and she had no thought for anything else. The situation of Claude was unknown to her, and her distress about her father's increasing weakness prevented her from thinking much about him. Her only hope now was, that on reaching the shore her father would experience a change for the better, and be benefited by the land air.

On removing Laborde from his berth, it was found that he not only had not strength to stand, but that he was even so weak that this motion served of itself to exhaust him fearfully. He had to be placed on a mattress, and carried in that way by four sailors to the ship's side, where he was carefully let down into the boat. There the mattress was placed in the boat's stern, and Laborde lay upon this, with his head supported against Mimi, who held him encircled in her arms. In this way he was taken ashore.

It was a long row, but the water was comparatively smooth, and the landing had been postponed until the flood tide, which made the boat's progress easier and swifter.

The nearest shore was very low, and the landing-place was two or three miles farther on. In the distance the land rose higher, and was covered with trees, with here and there a clearing. The land which they first approached was well wooded on the water side, but on passing this the whole scene changed. This land was an island, about two miles distant from the shore, with its inner side cleared, and dotted with houses and barns. Between this and the shore there extended a continuous tract of low land, which had evidently once been a salt-water marsh, for along the water's edge the coarse grass grew luxuriantly; but a little distance back there was a dike, about six or eight feet high, which ran from the island to the shore, and evidently protected the intervening level from the sea. The island itself thus served as a dike, and the artificial works that had been made ran where the sea had the least possible effect.

At length they approached the main land, and here they saw the low marsh-land all around them. Here a turbid river ran into the Basin, which came down a valley enclosed between wooded hills, and, with voluminous windings, terminated its course.

At this place there was a convenient beach for landing, and here Laborde was removed from the boat and carried up on the bank, where he was laid on his mattress under a shadowy willow tree. This point, though not very elevated, commanded a prospect which, to these new comers who had suffered so much from the sea, might have afforded the highest delight, had they been sufficiently free from care to take it all in. All around them lay one of the most fertile countries in all the world, and one of the most beautiful. The slopes of the hills rose in gentle acclivities, cultivated, dotted with groves and orchards, and lined with rows of tall poplars. The simple houses of the Acadian farmers, with their out-buildings, gave animation to the scene. At their feet lay a broad extent of dike-land, green and glowing with the verdure of June, spreading away to that island, which acted as a natural dike against the waters of the sea. Beyond this lay the blue waters of Minas Basin, on whose bosom floated the ship and the schooner, while in the distance rose the cliff which marked the entrance into the Basin, and all the enclosing shores.

But none of the party noticed this. Cazeneau was absorbed with his own plans; Laborde lay extended on the mattress, without any appearance of life except a faint breathing and an occasional movement; over him Mimi hung in intense anxiety, watching every change in his face, and filled with the most dreadful apprehensions; at a little distance stood Père Michel, watching them with sad and respectful sympathy.

Captain Ducrot had come ashore in the boat, and, leaving Laborde, he accompanied Cazeneau to a house which stood not far away. It was rather larger than the average, with a row of tall poplars in front and an orchard on one side. A road ran from the landing, past this house, up the hill, to the rest of the settlement farther on.

An old man was seated on a bench in the doorway. He rose as he saw the strangers, and respectfully removed his hat.

"How do you do, Robicheau?" said Ducrot. "You see I have come back again sooner than I expected. I have brought with me his excellency the governor of Louisbourg, who will be obliged if you can make him comfortable for a few days. Also there are the Count de Laborde and his daughter, whom I should like to bring here; but if you cannot make them comfortable, I can take them to Comeau's."

Upon this, Robicheau, with a low bow to Cazeneau, informed him that he thought there might be room for them all, if they would be willing to accept his humble hospitality. The old man spoke with much embarrassment, yet with sincere good will. He was evidently overwhelmed by the grandeur of his visitors, yet anxious to do all in his power to give them fitting entertainment. Ducrot now informed him that the Count de Laborde needed immediate rest and attention; whereupon Robicheau went in to summon his dame, who at once set to work to prepare rooms for the guests.

Ducrot now returned to the landing, and ordered the sailors to carry Laborde to Robicheau's house. They carried him on the mattress, supporting it on two oars, which were fastened with ropes in such a way as to form a very easy litter. Mimi walked by her father's side, while Père Michel followed in the rear. In this way they reached Robicheau's house. The room and the bed were already prepared, and Laborde was carried there. As he was placed upon that bed, Mimi looked at him with intense anxiety and alarm, for his pale, emaciated face and weak, attenuated frame seemed to belong to one who was at the last verge of life. An awful fear of the worst came over her — the fear of bereavement in this distant land, the presentiment of an appalling desolation, which crushed her young heart and reduced her to despair. Her father, her only relative, her only protector, was slipping away from her; and in the future there seemed nothing before her but the very blackness of darkness.

The good dame Robicheau saw her bitter grief, and shed tears of sympathy. She offered no word of consolation, for to her experienced eyes this feeble old man seemed already beyond the reach of hope. She could only show her compassion by her tears. Père Michel, also, had nothing to say; and to all the distress of the despairing young girl he could offer no word of comfort. It was a case where comfort could not be administered, and where the stricken heart could only be left to struggle with its own griefs — alone.

A few hours after the first boat went ashore, a second boat landed. By this time, a large number of the inhabitants had assembled at the landing-place, to see what was going on; for to these people the sight of a ship was a rare occurrence, and they all recognized the Aigle, and wondered why she had returned. This second boat carried Claude, who had thus been removed from the ship to the shore for the purpose of being conveyed to Louisbourg. Captain Ducrot and Cazeneau had already succeeded in finding a place where he could be kept. It was the house of one of the farmers of Grand Pré, named Comeau, one of the largest in the whole settlement.

Claude landed, and was committed to the care of Comeau, who had come down to receive his prisoner. It was not thought worth while to bind him, since, in so remote a place as this, there would be scarcely any inducement for him to try to escape. If he did so, he could only fly to the woods, and, as he could not support his life there, he would be compelled to return to the settlement, or else seek shelter and food among the Indians. In either case he would be recaptured; for the Acadians would all obey the order of the governor of Louisbourg, and deliver up to him any one whom he might designate; while the Indians would do the same with equal readiness, since they were all his allies. Under these circumstances, Claude was allowed to go with his hands free; and in this way he accompanied Comeau, to whose charge he was committed. He walked through the crowd at the landing without exciting any very particular attention, and in company with Comeau he walked for about half a mile, when he arrived at the house. Here he was taken to a room which opened into the general sitting-room, and was lighted by a small window in the rear of the house, and contained a bed and a chair. The door was locked, and Claude was left to his own reflections.

Left thus to himself, Claude did not find his own thoughts very agreeable. He could not help feeling that he was now, more than ever, in the power of the man who had shown himself so relentless and persevering in his enmity. He was far away from any one whom he could claim as a friend. The people here were evidently all the creatures of Ducrot and Cazeneau. He saw that escape was useless. To get away from this particular place of imprisonment might be possible, for the window could be opened, and escape thus effected; but, if he should succeed in flying, where could he go? Annapolis Royal was many miles away. He did not know the way there; he could not ask; and even if he did know the way, he could only go there by running the gantlet of a population who were in league with Cazeneau.

That evening, as old Comeau brought him some food, he tried to enter into conversation with him. He began in a gradual way, and as his host, or, rather, his jailer, listened, he went on to tell his whole story, insisting particularly on the idea that Cazeneau must be mistaken; for he thought it best not to charge him with deliberate malice. He hinted, also, that if he could escape he might bestow a handsome reward upon the man who might help him. To all this Comeau listened, and even gave utterance to many expressions of sympathy; but the end of it all was nothing. Either Comeau disbelieved him utterly, but was too polite to say so, or else he was afraid to permit the escape of the prisoner who had been intrusted to his care. Claude then tried another means of influencing him. He reminded him that the governor of Louisbourg had no jurisdiction here; that the Acadians of Grand Pré were subject to the King of England, and that all concerned in this business would be severely punished by the English as soon as they heard of it. But here Claude utterly missed his mark. No sooner had he said this, than old Comeau began to denounce the English with the utmost scorn and contempt. He told Claude that there were many thousands of French in Acadia, and only a hundred English; that they were weak and powerless; that their fort at Annapolis was in a ruinous state; and that, before another year, they would be driven out forever. He asserted that the King of France was the greatest of all kings; that France was the most powerful of all countries; that Louisbourg was the strongest fortress in the universe; and that the French would drive the English, not only out of Acadia, but out of America. In fact, Claude's allusion to the English proved to be a most unfortunate one; for, whereas at first the old man seemed to feel some sort of sympathy with his misfortunes, so, at the last, excited by this allusion, he seemed to look upon him as a traitor to the cause of France, and as a criminal who was guilty of all that Cazeneau had laid to his charge.

CHAPTER X.

ALONE IN THE WORLD.

THE condition of the old Count de Laborde grew steadily worse. The change to the land had done him no good, nor was all the loving care of Mimi of any avail whatever. Every one felt that he was doomed; and Mimi herself, though she struggled against that thought, still had in her heart a dark terror of the truth. This truth could at last be concealed no longer even from herself, for Père Michel came to administer the holy eucharist to the dying man, and to receive his last confession. Mimi could not be present while the dying man unfolded to his priest the secrets of his heart, nor could she hope to know what those secrets were. But dark indeed must they have been, and far, very far, beyond the scope of ordinary confessions, for the face of Père Michel, as he came forth from that room, was pale and sombre; and so occupied was he with his own thoughts that he took no notice of the weeping girl who stood there, longing to hear from him some word of comfort. But Père Michel had none to give. He left the house, and did not return till the next day.

By that time all was over. Laborde had passed away in the night. The priest went in to look upon the form of the dead. Mimi was there, bowed down in the deepest grief, for she felt herself all alone in the world. The priest stood looking at the face of the dead for some time with that same gloom upon his face which had been there on the preceding day, when he left that bedside. At length he turned to Mimi.

"Child," said he, in a voice full of pity, "I will not attempt to utter any words of condolence. I know well how the heart feels during the first emotions of sorrow over bereavement. Words are useless. I can only point you to Heaven, where all comfort dwells, and direct you to remember in your prayers him who lies here. The church is yours, with all her holy offices. The dearest friend must turn away from the dead, but the church remains, and follows him into the other world. Your heart may still be consoled, for you can still do something for the dear father whom you loved. You can pray for the soul of the departed, and thus it will seem to you as though you have not altogether lost him. He will seem near you yet when you pray for him; your spirit will seem to blend with his; his presence will seem about you. And besides, my dear child, this also I wish to say: you are not altogether alone in the world. I will watch over you till you go wherever you may wish. It is not much that I can do; but perhaps I can do for you all that you may now wish to be done for yourself. Think of this, then, dear child, and whenever you wish to have a friend's advice or assistance, come to me."

To this Mimi listened with streaming eyes; and as the priest ended, she pressed his hand gratefully, and uttered some unintelligible words. His offer had come to her like balm. It did not seem now as though she was so desolate, for she had learned already to love the good priest with something of a daughter's feelings, and to trust in him profoundly.

Laborde was buried in the little churchyard of Grand Pré; and now, in addition to the pangs of bereavement, Mimi began to feel other cares about her future. What was she to do? Could she go back to France? That was her only present course. But how? She could not go in the Aigle, for that frigate had left the day after her arrival, not having any time to spare. There was no other way of going to France now, except by going first to Louisbourg, and taking a ship from that place. But she was not left very long in suspense, for, two or three days after her father's burial, the Count de Cazeneau came to see her.

"I hope," he began, "that it is not necessary for me to say to you how deeply I sympathize with you in your bereavement, for I myself have my own bereavement to mourn over — the loss of my best, my only friend, the friend of a lifetime, the high-minded, the noble Laborde. The loss to me is irrevocable, and never can I hope to find any mere friend who may fill his place. We were always inseparable. We were congenial in taste and in spirit. My coming to America was largely due to his unfortunate resolve to come here, a resolve which I always combated to the best of my ability, and over which you and I must now mourn. But regrets are useless, and it remains for both of us to see about the future."

This somewhat formal opening was quite characteristic of Cazeneau, who, being of a distant, reserved nature, very seldom allowed himself to unbend; and, though he threw as much softness into his voice and manner as he was capable of using, yet Mimi felt repelled, and dreaded what might be coming.

"When we were first picked up by the Aigle," he continued, " it was in my power either to go direct to Louisbourg, or to come here, and then go on by land. I chose to come here, for two reasons; first, because I hoped that my dear friend would be benefited by reaching the land as soon as possible, and I thought that the pure, fresh air, and genial climate, and beautiful scenery of this lovely place would exercise upon him an immediate effect for the better. Another purpose which I had was an official one. I wished to see this place and this people with reference to my own administration and designs for the future. Unhappily, my hopes for my friend have proved unfounded, and my only consolation is that, though I have been disappointed as a private man in my affections, yet, as a public official, I have been able, during my short stay here, to do good service to my country, in a way which my country's enemies shall feel at a vital point before another year has passed away."

To this Mimi had nothing to say, for it was all preliminary, and she expected something more. She therefore waited in silence, though with much trepidation, to see what it might be that this man had in view with regard to her. Cazeneau then continued: —

"As I have now done all that I intended to do in this place, it is my intention to set forth for Louisbourg by land. I have some faithful Indians as guides, and the journey is not very fatiguing. In Louisbourg you will be able to obtain every comfort, and there will be friends and associates for you, your own social equals, who may make your life pleasanter than it has been for a long time."

By this Cazeneau directly stated his intention of taking Mimi with him to Louisbourg — a statement which did not surprise Mimi, for it was what she had expected. Now, however, that he said this, and in this way, without pretending to ask her consent, her trepidation increased, and she thought with terror over that long and lonely journey, which she would have to make with this man and a band of savages. There was nothing else, however, to be done. She could neither hope nor desire to remain in Grand Pré. Her position was a painful one, and the only hope remaining was that of returning to France. And to go to Louisbourg was the surest way of doing that. One thing, however, she could not help asking, for this she felt to be a matter of extreme importance.

"Is Père Michel going?"

"He is," said Cazeneau. "He has asked permission to go with our party, and I have granted it."

At this answer a great relief was felt by Mimi, and the future seemed less dark.

"I have granted it," said Cazeneau, "because he seems a harmless man, and may be useful in various ways to me, hereafter, in my plans. He seems to know the people about here. I dare say he's been here before.

"Your position at Louisbourg," continued Cazeneau, "will be one which will be most honorable: as the daughter of the Count de Laborde, you will receive universal attention, and my influence shall be exerted to make everything contribute to your happiness. As commandant, I shall, of course, be supreme; my house will be like a small vice-regal court, and the little world of Louisbourg will all do homage to any one whom I may hold up before them as a worthy object."

Cazeneau paused after he had said this. It was a speech which was uttered slowly and with emphasis, but its meaning was not altogether apparent to Mimi. Still there was enough of it intelligible to her to make it seem excessively unpleasant. What he exactly meant was of no importance, the general meaning being certainly this: that he designed for her some prolonged stay there, during which he intended to secure homage and respect for her. Now, that was a thing that Mimi recoiled from with distaste. She had always detested this man, she had always shrunk from him. Her present position of dependence was most bitter; but to have that position continue was intolerable. It was as though he tried to put himself into the place of her beloved father, — he, whom she regarded as her father's evil genius, — as though he intended to make himself her guardian, and introduce her as his ward.

"You speak," said she, in a trembling voice, "just as — as if — I — you supposed that I was going to live at Louisbourg."

"And where else do you wish to live?" asked Cazeneau, placidly.

"I want to go home," said Mimi, her eyes filling with tears, and her voice sounding like the wail of a child that has lost its way.

"My poor child," said Cazeneau, more tenderly than he had yet spoken, "you evidently do not understand your position as yet. I did not intend to say anything about it; but, since you feel this way, and have spoken so, I suppose I must make some explanation.

Well, then, my poor child, when your father left France on this unfortunate errand, he turned all his property into money, expecting to use that money in America in some way, in that mysterious design of his which brought him out here. All this money was on board the Arethuse with him, and it is hardly necessary to say that it was all lost. I know that his grief over this, and the thought that he was leaving you penniless, did more to shorten his life than the sufferings which he had on the sea. He sank under it. He told me that he could not rally from it; and it was his utter hopelessness that made him give way so completely. So, my poor child, this is your present situation: your father's estates are sold, and are now in the hands of strangers; your father's money is now at the bottom of the Atlantic Ocean; so that to return to France is, for the present, at least, not to be thought of.

"For my part," continued Cazeneau, as Mimi sat there dumb with horror at hearing this fresh and crushing news, "I do not see anything in your situation which need give you one moment's uneasiness. You have lost your father, but your father's best friend still lives, and he will never see the daughter of his friend know one single trouble, if he can help it. We were more than brothers. Suppose you try to think of me with something of the same confidence that your father felt. I, for my part, will put you in his place. You shall never know a care. You may consider yourself rich. You shall have no trouble except that deep sorrow which you feel as a fond daughter."

"I cannot live in America," moaned Mimi, despairingly, recoiling in her heart from Cazeneau, and dreading him more than ever. "I cannot. I want to go home; or, if I have no home, I want to go to France. I will enter a convent."

Cazeneau smiled at this.

"Such a wish, dear child," said he, " is quite natural now, in the first freshness of your bereâvement; but time alleviates all sorrow, and you may think differently hereafter. As to returning to France, you shall most certainly do that. I intend to go back after a time; and you will once more live in our dear, native land. But, for the present, let us not talk of these things. Louisbourg is now our destination. Fear nothing. You shall not know a care. You shall be guarded from every want, and every wish shall be gratified. You shall find yourself surrounded by the most anxious, and tender, and solicitous care for your happiness."

These last words were spoken in a warmer and more impassioned manner than Cazeneau had thus far used, and their effect upon Mimi was so much the more unpleasant. He then raised her hand to his lips with respectful affection, and took his departure.

Mimi was for a time quite overwhelmed. The sorrow which she had experienced for her father gave way to a new feeling — one of terror, deep, dark, and irremovable — about herself and her own future. All Cazeneau's words recurred to her, and the more she thought of them, the more hateful did they seem. Out of them all several things appeared plain to her mind.

First, that she was a pauper. Of Cazeneau's words she did not doubt the truth. It seemed in the highest degree probable. She had all along known that her father had come to America to search after some of the Montresors, and to made reparation. Cazeneau now had informed her that he had turned all his property into money. It must have been for that purpose. The thought had never occurred to her before; but, now that it was stated, she did not dream of doubting it. It seemed too true.

Secondly, she saw that Cazeneau, for some reason or other, was determined to keep her under his control. He was determined not to allow her to return to France, and not to enter a convent. He was bent upon associating her with his own life, and causing her to be admired in Louisbourg. Added to this was his promise to take her back to France with himself. All this showed that he would on no account allow her to part with him. What was the meaning of it all? And now the thought could no longer be kept out of her mind: Cazeneau's purpose was to make her his wife.

His wife!

The thought was to her most odious; but, having once presented itself, she could not argue it away, nor could she get rid of it at all. Yes, that was the meaning that lurked behind his words all the time. That was the meaning of his promise to make her admired and happy.

Finally, she remembered how he had stated to her the fact that he was supreme in Louisbourg, and that through his grandeur she was to receive homage from all the lesser throng. To her this seemed like a plain statement that she was in his power, and entirely at his mercy.

And now, what could she do? The future was worse than ever. She was completely in the power of a man whom she detested — a man upon whom she looked as her father's evil genius, as one whose evil counsel had long ago led her father to that act which he had atoned for by remorse and death. She was now in the hands of this villain. Escape seemed impossible. He was supreme here. From him there was no appeal. And she was a beggar. But, even if she were rich, what hope could she have against him?

As she asked herself this question, there was no answer. She did not know what she could do, and could scarcely hope that she would ever know.

It was in this state of mind that Père Michel found her, on the evening of that day. Mimi saw his arrival with intense delight. Here seemed one who might relieve her in her distress. Accordingly she proceeded to tell him her whole story, all the words of Cazeneau, with all their implied meaning, and all her own fears, from beginning to end.

The priest heard her narration in profound silence, and after she had told him all, he remained in deep thought for some time, while Mimi sat anxiously awaiting what he might say.

"My dear child," said the priest, at length, "it is difficult for me to give you advice, for your situation is most unpleasant, and most distressing to me. I can only entreat you to put your trust in that Heaven who never deserts the innocent. You must go to Louisbourg — there is no hope of escaping that. Besides, you yourself wish to go there. The Count de Cazeneau certainly has the chief power there; but whether he is omnipotent remains to be seen. Who knows what other powers may be there? I have known cases where the commandant has had powerful rivals,

— such as the admiral of the fleet, or some subordinate who had influence at court at home. I have known places where the bishop could interfere and prevent his doing wrong. So, be calm, my daughter, put your trust in Heaven, and recollect that the commandant cannot break through all restraints, but that there must be some barriers that he cannot force. If you wish the protection of the church, that will always be yours. Beware how you do anything rashly. Confide in me. Perhaps, after all, these troubles may have a good end."

CHAPTER XI.

A FRIEND IN NEED.

FOR more than a week Claude had been kept in confinement, and had seen nothing of any of his former acquaintances. The confinement was not so close as it might have been, and escape was not absolutely impossible, for the window which lighted the chamber was merely a wooden sash, with four panes of glass, which Claude could have removed, had he been so disposed; but this he was not inclined to do, and for two reasons. One reason was, because, if he did get out, he had no idea where to go. Annapolis Royal was the nearest settlement belonging to the English; but he did not know in which direction it lay. He knew, however, that between Grand Pré and that place the country was settled by the French, among whom he could not go without being captured by his pursuers, while if he took to the woods he would be sure to fall into the hands of the Indians, who were the zealous allies of the French. Such a prospect was of itself sufficient to deter him from the attempt to escape. But there was also another reason. He could not bear the thought of leaving Mimi forever, and never seeing her again. If he should succeed in escaping to Annapolis Royal, it would be an eternal separation between her and himself. Grand Pré seemed pleasant to him since she was here; and he thought it better to be a prisoner here than a free man elsewhere. He, therefore, deliberately preferred to run any risk that might be before him, with the faint hope of seeing Mimi again, rather than to attempt flight.

What had happened since he had come here he did not know very clearly. From conversation which he had overheard he had gathered that Laborde was dead; but, when he asked any of them about it, they refused to tell him anything at all. Claude was, therefore, left to make the most that he could out of this vague information. But the intelligence caused him to feel much anxiety about Mimi. He remembered well all that she had ever told him, and could not help wondering what she would do under present circumstances. Would she be willing to remain in the neighborhood of Cazeneau? But how could she help it? Would not Cazeneau take advantage of her present loneliness to urge forward any plans that he might have about her?

Already the suspicion had come to Claude that Cazeneau had certain plans about Mimi. What he thought was this: that Laborde was rich, that Mimi was his heiress, and that Cazeneau was a man of profligate life and ruined fortunes, who was anxious to repair his fortunes by marrying this heiress. To such a man the disparity in their years would make no difference, nor would he particularly care whether Mimi loved him or not, so long as he could make her his wife, and gain control over her property. What had given him this idea about Cazeneau's position and plans it is difficult to say; but it was probably his own jealous fears about Mimi, and his deep detestation of his enemy.

And now he began to chafe against the narrow confines of his chamber with greater impatience. He longed to have some one with whom he could talk. He wondered whether Cazeneau would remain here much longer, and, if he went away, whether he would take Mimi or leave her. He wondered, also, whether he would be taken to Louisbourg. He felt as if he would rather go there, if Mimi was to go, even at the risk of his life, than remain behind after she had left. But all his thoughts and wonders resulted in nothing whatever, for it was impossible to create any knowledge out of his own conjectures.

He was in the midst of such thoughts as these when his ears were attracted by the sound of a familiar voice. He listened attentively. It was the voice of Père Michel. No sooner had Claude satisfied himself that it was indeed the priest, than he felt sure that he had come here to visit him; and a little longer waiting showed that this was the case. There were advancing footsteps. Madame Comeau opened the door, and Père Michel entered the chamber. The door was then shut, and the two were alone.

So overcome was Claude by joy that he flung himself into the priest's arms and embraced him. The good priest seemed to reciprocate his emotion, for there were tears in his eyes, and the first words that he spoke were in tremulous tones.

"My son," the priest commenced, in gentle, paternal tones, and in a voice that was tremulous with emotion, "you must calm yourself." Then, suddenly speaking in English, he said, "It is necessaire dat we sall spik Ingeles, for ze peuple of ze house may suspeck —"

Upon this Claude poured forth a torrent of questions in English, asking about Laborde, Cazeneau, Zac, and Mimi. It will not be necessary to report the words of the priest in his broken English, but rather to set them down according to the sense of them. So the priest said, —

"You speak too fast, my son. One thing at a time. The poor Laborde is dead and buried. The Count Cazeneau is about to go to Louisbourg. Mimi is going with him."

"Mimi going with him!" cried Claude, in deep agitation.

"Be calm, my son. Do not speak so loud. I have told the people of this house that your life is in danger, and that I have come as a priest, to hear your last confession. I do not wish them to suspect my real errand. We may talk as we wish, only do not allow yourself to be agitated."

"But tell me," said Claude, in a calmer voice, "how is it possible that Mimi can trust herself with Cazeneau?"

"*Ma foi*," said the priest, "it is possible, for she cannot help it. But do not fear. I am going to accompany them, and, as far as my feeble power can do anything, I will watch over her, and see that she suffers no injustice. I hope that Heaven will assist her innocence and my protection; so do not allow yourself to be uneasy about her; but hope for the best, and trust in Heaven."

At this Claude was silent for a few moments. At length he said, —

"O, Père Michel, must I stay here when she goes? Can you tell me what they are going to do with me?"

"It is about yourself that I am going to speak, and it was for this that I came," said the priest.

"Can I go with the others to Louisbourg?" asked Claude, eagerly; for he thought only of being near Mimi.

"Heaven forbid!" said the priest. "It is in a far different way that you are to go. Listen to me. The Count de Cazeneau is going to set out to-morrow, with a party of Indians as escort. Mimi is to be taken with him. I am going, too. It is his intention to leave you here for a time, till his escort can return. They will then take you to Louisbourg. If he can find any Indians on the way whom he can make use of, he will send them here for you. But meantime you are to be kept imprisoned here.

"Now, I am acquainted with the Indians better than most men. I lived in Acadie formerly, long enough to be well known to the whole tribe. I am also well known to the Acadians. Among the Indians and the Acadians there are many who would willingly lay down their lives for me. I could have delivered you before this, but I saw that you were not in any immediate danger; so I preferred postponing it until the Count de Cazeneau had left. I do not wish him to suspect that I have any interest in you; and when he hears of your escape, I do not wish him to think that I had anything to do with it. But I have already made all the plans that are necessary, and the men are in this neighborhood with whom I have arranged for your escape."

"What is the plan?" asked Claude, eagerly.

"I will tell you," said the priest. "There are six Indians, all of them devoted to me. They will guide you to a place of safety, and will be perfectly faithful to you as long as they are with you. They are ready to go anywhere with you, to do anything for you, even to the extent of laying down their lives for you. It is for my sake that they are willing to show this devotion. I have presented you to them as my representative, and they look upon you as they would look upon me. But, first of all, you are to get out of this. Can you open that window?"

"It was fastened tight when I first came," said Claude; "but I have loosened it, so that I can take it out very quickly."

"Very good. Now, one of these Indians will be here to-morrow night. We shall leave to-morrow morning; and I do not want you to be rescued till after our departure. At midnight, to-morrow, then, the Indian will be here. He will give a sound like a frog, immediately outside, under the window. You must then open the window. If you see him, or hear him, you must then get out, and he will take you to the woods. After that he and the rest of the Indians will take you through the woods to Port Royal, which they call Annapolis Royal. Here you will be safe from Cazeneau until such time as may suit you to go back to Boston. Annapolis Royal is about twenty-four leagues from this place, and you can easily go there in two days."

Claude listened to all this without a word; and, after the priest had ended, he remained silent for some time, with his eyes fixed on the floor.

"The Indians will be armed," said the priest, "and will have a rifle and a sword for you. So you need have no trouble about anything."

"My dear Père Michel," said Claude, at last, "you lay me under very great obligations; but will you not add to them by allowing me to select my own route?"

"Your own route?" asked the priest. "What do you mean? You don't know the country, especially the woods, while these Indians will be at home there."

"What I mean is this," said Claude: "will you not allow me the use of this Indian escort in another direction than the one you mention?"

"Another direction? Why, where else can you possibly go? Annapolis is the nearest place for safety."

"I should very much prefer," said Claude "to go to Canso."

"To Canso!" said the priest, in great surprise; "to Canso! Why, you would come on our track!"

"That is the very reason why I wish to go there. Once in Canso, I should be as safe as in Annapolis."

The priest shook his head.

"From what I hear, Canso cannot be a safe place for you very long. England and France are on the eve of war, and Cazeneau expects to get back Acadie — a thing that is very easy for him to do. But why do you wish to venture so near to Louisburg? Cazeneau will be there now; and it will be a very different place from what it would have been had you not saved Cazeneau from the wreck, and made him your enemy."

"My dear Père Michel," said Claude, "I will be candid with you. The reason why I wish to go in that direction is for the sake of being near to Mimi, and on account of the hope I have that I may rescue her."

"Mimi! Rescue her!" exclaimed the priest, astonished, not at the young man's feelings towards Mimi, for those he had already discovered, but rather at the boldness of his plan, — "rescue her! Why how can you possibly hope for that, when she will be under the vigilant eye of Cazeneau?"

"I will hope it, at any rate," said Claude. "Besides, Cazeneau will not be vigilant, as he will not suspect that he is followed. His Indians will suspect nothing. I may be able, by means of my Indians, to entice her away, especially if you prepare her mind for my enterprise."

The priest was struck by this, and did not have any argument against it; yet the project was evidently distasteful to him.

"It's madness," said he. "My poor boy, it may cost you your life."

"Very well," said Claude; "let it go. I'd rather not live, if I can't have Mimi."

The priest looked at him sadly and solemnly.

"My poor boy," said he, "has it gone so far as that with you?"

"As far as that — yes," said Claude, "and farther. Recollect I saved her life. It seems to me as if Heaven threw her in my way; and I'll not give her up without striking a blow. Think of that scoundrel Cazeneau. Think of the danger she is in while under his power. There is no hope for her if he once gets her in Louisbourg; the only hope for her is before she reaches that place; and the only one who can save her is myself. Are my Indians faithful for an enterprise of that kind?"

"I have already told you," said the priest, "that they would all lay down their lives for you. They will go wherever you lead. And now, my dear son," continued the priest, "I did not think that you would dream of an enterprise like this. But, since you have made the proposal, and since you are so earnest about it, why, I make no opposition. I say, come, in Heaven's name. Follow after us; and, if you can come up with us, and effect a communication with Mimi, do so. Your Indians must be careful; and you will find that they can be trusted in a matter of this kind. If I see that you are coming up with us, and find any visitors from you, I will prepare Mimi for it. But suppose you succeed in rescuing her," added the priest; "have you thought what you would do next?"

"No," said Claude; "nor do I intend to think about that. It will depend upon where I am. If I am near Canso, I shall go there, and trust to finding some fisherman; if not, I shall trust to my Indians to take us back through the woods to Annapolis. But there's one thing that you might do."

"What?"

"Zac — is he on board the schooner, or ashore?"

"The skipper?" said the priest. "No. I have not seen him. I think he must be aboard the schooner. It is my intention to communicate with him before I leave this place."

"Do so," said Claude, eagerly; "and see if you can't get him free, as you have managed for me; and if you can persuade him, or beg him for me, to sail around to Canso, and meet me there, all will be well. That is the very thing we want. If he will only promise to go there, I will push on to Canso myself, at all hazards."

The priest now prepared to go. A few more words

were exchanged, after which Claude and Père Michel embraced. The priest kissed him on both cheeks.

"Adieu, my dear son," said he. "I hope we may meet again."

"Adieu, dear Père Michel," said Claude. "I shall never forget your kindness."

With this farewell the two separated; the priest went out, and the door was fastened again upon Claude.

For the remainder of that night, Claude did not sleep much. His mind was filled with the new prospect that the priest's message had opened before him. The thought of being free once more, and at the head of a band of devoted followers, on the track of Mimi, filled him with excitement. That he would be able to overtake the party of Cazeneau, he did not doubt; that he would be able to rescue Mimi, he felt confident. The revulsion from gloom and despondency to hope and joy was complete, and the buoyant nature of Claude made the transition an easy one. It was with difficulty that he could prevent himself from bursting forth into songs. But this would have been too dangerous, since it would have attracted the attention of the people of the house, and led them to suspect that the priest had spoken other words to him than those of absolution; or they might report this sudden change to Cazeneau, and thereby excite his suspicions.

The next day came. Claude knew that on this day Cazeneau and his party had left, for he overheard the people of the house speaking about it. According to their statements, the party had left at about four in the morning. This filled Claude with a fever of impatience, for he saw that this first day's march would put them a long way ahead, and make it difficult for him to catch up with them. But there was only one day, and he tried to comfort himself with the thought that he could travel faster than the others, and also that the priest and Mimi would both manage to retard their progress, so as to allow him to catch up.

The day passed thus, and evening came at last. Hour after hour went by. All the family retired, and the house was still. Claude then slowly, and carefully, and noiselessly removed the window from its place. Then he waited. The hours still passed on. At last he know that it must be about midnight.

Suddenly he heard, immediately outside, a low, guttural sound — the well-known sound of a frog. It was the signal mentioned by the priest. The time had come.

He put his head cautiously outside. Crouched there against the wall of the house, close underneath, he saw a dusky figure. A low, whispered warning came up. Claude responded in a similar manner. Then, softly and noiselessly, he climbed out of the window. His feet touched the ground. No one had heard him. He was saved.

CHAPTER XII.

THE PARSON AMONG THE PHILISTINES.

A MAP of this part of America, in this year, 1743, would show a very different scene from that which is presented by one of the present date. The country held by the English did not reach beyond the Kennebec, although claimed by them. But north of this river it was all in the virtual possession of the French, and on the map it was distinguished by the French colors. A line drawn from the mouth of the Penobscot, due north, to the River St. Lawrence, divided New England from the equally extensive territory of New Scotland, or Nova Scotia. This New England was bordered on the east by Nova Scotia, on the north by the River St. Lawrence, and on the west by the province of New York. But in New England the French colors prevailed over quite one half of this territory; and in Nova Scotia, though all was claimed by the English, every part was actually held by the French, except one or two points of a most unimportant character.

Looking over such a map, we perceive the present characteristics all gone, and a vast wilderness, full of roaming tribes of Indians, filling the scene. North of Boston there are a few towns; but beyond the little town of Falmouth, the English settlements are all called

Fort this and Fort that. Up the valley of the Kennebec is the mark of a road to Quebec; and about half way, at the head waters of the Kennebec, a point is marked on the map with these words: "*Indian and French rendezvous. Extremely proper for a fort, which would restrain the French and curb the Abenakki Indians.*" And also: "*From Quebec to Kennebek River mouth, not much above half way to Boston, and one third to New York, thence by that R. and ye Chaudiere ye road to Canada is short.*"

North of the St. Lawrence is a vast country, which is called New France. As Old France and Old England struggle for the supremacy in the old world, so New France and New England struggle for the supremacy in the new world, and the bone of contention is this very district alluded to, — this border-ground, — called by the French L'Acadie, but claimed by the English as Nova Scotia, which bordered both on New England and New France.

This debatable territory on the map is full of vast waste spaces, together with the names of savage tribes never heard of before or since, some of which are familiar names, merely spelled in an unusual manner, while others owe their origin, perhaps, to the imagination of the map-maker or his informant. Thus, for example, we have Massasuk, Arusegenticook, Saga Dahok, and others of equally singular sound.

In this debatable territory are numerous forts, both French and English. These are situated, for the most part, in the valleys of rivers, for the very good reason that these valleys afford the best places for settlement, and also for the further reason that they are generally used as the most convenient routes of travel by those who go by land from one post to another. These forts are numerous on the west of New England; they also stud the map in various places towards the north. The valley of the St. John, in Nova Scotia, is marked by several of these. Farther on, the important isthmus which connects the peninsula of Nova Scotia with the main land is protected by the strong post called Fort Beausejour.

In this peninsula of Nova Scotia, various settlements are marked. One is named Minas, which is also known as Grand Pré, a large and important community, situated in one of the most beautiful and fertile valleys in America. In the neighborhood of this are a half dozen points, marked with the general name of French settlements, while the vacant places between and beyond are marked with the name Mic Macs, which is the title of the Indians who inhabit Nova Scotia. One post here, however, possesses a singular interest in the eyes of the good people of Boston. It is marked on the map by the name of Annapolis, once the French Port Royal, but now the only English post of any consequence in all Nova Scotia. Here resides the handful of Englishmen who claim to rule the province. But the government is a mockery, and the French set it at defiance. If England wishes to assert her power here, she must have a far different force in the country from the handful of ragged and ill-armed soldiers who mount guard on the tumble-down forts at Annapolis.

Beyond all these, at the extreme east of the peninsula, is an island called by the French Ile Royale, and by the English Cape Breton. This is held by the French. Here is their greatest stronghold in America, except Quebec, and one, too, which is regarded by

Boston with greater jealousy and dread than the latter, since it is actually nearer, is open winter and summer, and can strike a more immediate blow.

This was the extreme eastern outpost of French power in America. Here the French colonies reached out their arms to the mother country. Here began that great chain of fortresses, which ran up the valleys of navigable rivers, and connected with the great fortress of Quebec the almost impregnable outpost of Ticonderoga, and the posts of Montreal Island. From these the chain of military occupation extended itself towards the south, through the valleys of the Ohio and the Mississippi, until they were connected with the flourishing colony at New Orleans.

Thus it was, and with these advantages, that the French engaged in the great and momentous conflict with the English for the possession of America, and on the side of the former were the greater part of the wild and warlike Indians.

And now let us return to our friend Zac, who for some time has been lost sight of.

When the Aigle came to anchor, the schooner did the same, and lay under her guns some miles out from the shore. Zac had been allowed a certain amount of freedom, for, as the lieutenant had promised, his hands had not been bound. The same liberty was allowed to the others on board. Six French seamen were on board, who navigated the schooner, and acted as her guard. These were armed, while Zac and his friends were all unarmed. While sailing up the bay this guard was hardly necessary, as the schooner was under the guns of the frigate; but afterwards the necessity was more apparent.

The Aigle could not wait at Grand Pré longer than was requisite to land those who were going ashore. The boat that landed these brought back a half dozen Acadians from Grand Pré, whom it left on board the schooner. Then, taking back again her own seamen, the Aigle spread her white wings and sailed away for *La Belle France.*

Zac saw this change in affairs with varied feelings. First of all, he had half hoped that he might be let off, after all; partly because it was not a time of formal war, and partly because the schooner had saved some important lives, and therefore, at the very least, ought to be let off. But this change in her masters dispelled Zac's hope, and made him see that there was not at all any prospect of an immediate release. From that moment Zac gave up all hope of any release whatever, and began to see that, if escape were to be made, it must be effected by his own skill and daring.

The new comers seemed willing to maintain the old state of things, and showed no inclination to keep their prisoners in bonds. They were a good-natured lot, with simple, unsophisticated faces, and looked with amiable smiles upon the schooner and its company. Still, they were all stout, able-bodied fellows, and all were armed. The leader was a man of about forty, who seemed to be regarded by the rest with considerable respect. He was also able to speak a few words of English. They contented themselves with keeping a general lookout over the schooner and its crew, and taking turns at the night watch.

In fact, the simple confidence of the Acadians in the security of their guard seemed to be justified by circumstances. These six stout men were armed; Zac·

and his followers were unarmed. All the floating craft in the Basin belonged to the Acadians, and all the settlements. For Zac to escape by water was scarcely possible, and to get off by land was not to be thought of. The nearest English settlement was many miles away, and to reach it he would have to run the gantlet of a population of French and Indians.

Day after day passed, and Zac spent most of the time in meditating over his situation and keeping his eyes and ears on the alert. He understood pretty well that to the villany of Cazeneau were due both his own captivity and the more serious danger which threatened his friend. It was from Margot that he had first heard of Cazeneau as an enemy, and little more had he been able to find out beyond what she had told him in the brief conversation already related. The illness of Laborde had necessitated her attendance on her master and mistress, and prevented any further confidences. Only a few occasional greetings were possible after that. Then followed the arrival of the Aigle, and the transfer of Margot, with the rest, to the French frigate. Zac had consequently been left in the dark as to the particular villany of Cazeneau towards Laborde and Mimi. But he had seen enough and felt enough to be sure that his enmity, from whatever cause it arose, was of no common kind, that Claude was in great danger, and that he himself was involved in the same peril, though to a less degree. This conviction served, therefore, to keep his mind continually on the alert, so as to find out what was the present situation of Claude, and also to devise and lay hold of some plan of action for himself.

In his thoughts the good Père Michel was suggested

as the only one who could do anything for either of them. What his influence might be, he could not guess; but he at least believed in his friendliness and good faith, and he could not help feeling that the priest would do all that was possible. It seemed to him not unlikely that the priest might come out to see him, and convey to him some information about the present state of affairs in Grand Pré. And besides this, he could not help feeling a vague hope that, even if the priest were unable to do anything, he might receive some sort of a message from one whom he could not help as regarding in the light of a friend — namely, the amiable Margot.

The situation had been accepted by the rest of the ship's company without any great display of emotion. Biler's melancholy remained unchanged, and still, as of yore, he passed much of his time at the mast-head, contemplating the universe, and eating raw turnips. Jericho remained as busy as ever, and cared for his pots, and his kettles, and his pans, without apparently being conscious that his master was a slave now, as well as himself. Upon Terry, also, the yoke of captivity lay but lightly. It was not in the nature of Terry to be downcast or sullen; and the simple expedients which had led him to fraternize with the shipwrecked sailors had afterwards enabled him to fraternize equally well with the crew of the Aigle that had been put on board. These had gone, and it remained now for him to come to an understanding with the Acadians. Constant practice had made him more capable, and, in addition to his own natural advantages, he had also learned a few French words, of which he made constant use in the most efficient way. The Acadians responded to Terry's advances quite as readily as any of the others had done; and before they had been on board one day they were all singing and laughing with the merry Irish lad, and going into fits of uproarious mirth at Terry's incessant use of the few French words which he had learned; for it was Terry's delight to stop each one of them, and insist on shaking hands, whenever he met them, saying at the same time, with all the gravity in the world, —

"*Commy voo porty voo, bong tong. Bon jure, moosoo!*"

Thus nearly a week passed, and during all that time Zac had heard nothing about the fate of his friends ashore. Neither the priest nor Margot sent him any message whatever. The Acadians themselves did not hold any communication with the shore, but remained on board quite placidly, in a state of calm content — as placidly, indeed, as though they had been living on board the Parson all their lives.

During all the time Zac had been meditating over his situation, and trying to see his way out of it. At length a ray of light began to dawn into his mind, which illuminated his present position, and opened up to him a way of action. One day after dinner, while the Acadians were lolling in the sun, and while Terry was smoking his pipe forward, Zac sauntered up to him in a careless fashion, and placing himself near Terry, where he could not be overheard, he began to talk in an easy tone with the other,

"Terry, lad," said he, "I'm getting tired o' this here."

"Faix, an' it's mesilf that's been waitin' to hear ye say that same for a week an' more — so it is."

"I THINK THAT WE CAN MANAGE TO GET THE SCHOONER FROM THESE CHAPS." Page 188.

"Wal, ye see, I ben a turnin' it over in my mind, and hain't altogether seen my way clear afore; but now it seems to me as how it's a burnin' shame to stand this here any longer."

"Thrue for you; an' so it is," said Terry. "An' so, ef ye've got anythin' on yer mind that ye want to do, why, out with it, for I'm your man."

"Wal, ye see," resumed Zac, "it's this here; I don't want to go away out o' this jest yet."

"Not go away! Tare an ages," cried Terry; "d'ye want to be a prisoner?"

"Course not. I mean this: I don't want to go an' leave my friend here, Motier, in the hands of the Philistines."

"Sure ye can't do anythin' for him; an' he's among his own kin — so he is; for he jabbers French ayqual to the best of thim."

"No, I can't do anything for him as I am; that's a fact; and so I'm bound to put myself in a position whar I can do somethin'; that is, I'm bound to seize this here schewner, an' bring the old Parson back to the fold."

"Arrah, sure, an' that's the right sort of talk — so it is; an' it's mesilf that's glad to hear ye. An' so, what is it, captain dear? Out with it. Tell me what yer plan is, an' I'm wid ye — so I am."

"I think, Terry, that we can manage to get the schewner from these chaps — can't we?"

"Sure we can. Sure, an' I'd ingage to do it alone, almost."

"They don't watch much."

"Not a bit of it."

"The two that watch at night sleep half the time."

"Sure, an' that's thrue for you, for I've seed thim at it whin I was asleep mesilf."

"We can git Jericho to bar down the cabin door, Terry, an' then you an' I can seize the two on deck."

"Aisy enough — so it is. They'll all be dead asleep — so they will."

"Wal, thar we'll have them; an' then I hope to be able to bring a pressure on the natyves of these regions by which I may git my friend out of their clutches."

"Sure, an' I don't onderstand ye at all, at all."

"Why, I'll have these six Acadians prisoners, an' then I'll sail up off Grand Pré, an' threaten to cut the throats of all of them if they don't send off Motier to me in ten minutes."

"Tare an' ages!" cried Terry. "Whoroo! but isn't that the plan? It is. It bates the wurruld — so it does. An whin'll ye begin, captain darlint?"

"To-night," said Zac.

CHAPTER XIII.

A STROKE FOR LIBERTY.

ZAC and Terry talked for a long time over the plan, trying to chat in an off-hand and careless manner, so as not to excite any suspicion. No suspicion appeared to be raised among the Acadians, who took no notice of them whatever. So Zac and Terry had sufficient opportunity to arrange all the details of the plan, and it was decided that Terry should indicate to Jericho what was to be done by him. It was agreed that the best time would be about three o'clock in the morning; for then the Acadians below would all be in their soundest sleep, while those who kept watch on deck would probably, in accordance with their usual careless fashion, be sunk into a slumber no less sound. Terry at length left Zac, and moved about in a desultory fashion, after which he finally settled down among the Acadians, and began to sing to them the immortal strain of St. Patrick.

Although Zac had upon his mind the weight of such an important enterprise, yet it did not at all interfere with his usual slumbers. He went to bed at nine, and slept soundly. At about half past two he awoke, and waited a little longer. Then he roused Terry and Jericho. Terry then went upon deck noiselessly, and reconnoitred. It was as they had hoped it would be.

Two men were on deck as a watch, but both were crouched under the taffrail fast asleep. Terry proposed to go and shut down the cabin door, where the rest of the Acadians were; but Zac concluded that it would be best for Jericho to do this, so that in case the noise should wake the watch, he and Terry might be on hand to deal with them. Jericho was now sent aft, charged with the burden of an important commission. He went softly and swiftly, like a spirit of night. His whole nature seemed changed by the purpose before him. In an instant he had ceased to be the lowly slave intent on cookery, and had started up into the attitude of an African warrior. As he glided along, Zac and Terry, with equal noiselessness, moved towards the slumbering watch, and then waited. It was necessary that the cabin should first be closed, so that those within, if alarmed by the outcry of their friends, should not be able to help them.

All went on well. Jericho reached the cabin, and then swiftly, and with as little noise as possible, shut the door and fastened it. Upon this, Zac and Terry each seized one of the slumbering Acadians, and before they were fairly awake they were disarmed.

Zac and Terry both scorned to bind them, partly out of kindly feeling towards them, partly because they themselves had not been bound, and partly out of the pride of their manhood. The Acadians at first stood stupefied, and then, recognizing the whole truth, they slunk forward, and stood dejectedly in the bows, where they awaited with fear the further action of their late prisoners.

Both Terry and Zac made friendly signs to them, pressing their hands on their hearts, smiling, nodding, and so forth; while Terry even went so far as to whistle one of their favorite melodies. But the Acadians were not to be reassured. They looked upon themselves as lost men, and evidently regarded Terry as a traitor of the deepest dye.

They now waited till the others in the cabin should make some sign. Jericho had armed himself with an axe, with which he stood ready to act in case of a fight. It was evident that the Acadians in the cabin had heard nothing whatever, and not one of them awaked before the usual time. Then, of course, the painful discovery was made by them. At first, loud cries and threats were made; but these were stilled by Zac, who in a voice of thunder awed them into silence.

"You are prisoners!" said he. "Give up your arms."

The one who understood a little English was able to comprehend this. The command was followed by an excited debate among the four, which was at last ended by a second mandate from Zac, accompanied by a threat to fire upon them. At this a hurried answer was given:—

"We render. We render. Fire not."

A small skylight was then opened, and all the arms and equipments of the prisoners were passed up. These were appropriated by Zac. The door of the cabin was then unfastened and opened, and the prisoners called upon to come forth. They came looking fearful and dejected, as though apprehending the worst. Zac, Terry, and Jericho, each with his musket, stood at the stern, and as they came out they motioned to them to go to the bows. The Acadians obeyed in silence, and soon joined their two companions.

Some time was now occupied by Zac in talking over with Terry the best course to be pursued. They at length decided to allow the Acadians to remain unbound by day, and to shut them down at night, or while sailing. As long as these men were unarmed and themselves armed, they had not the slightest fear of any trouble arising. For the Acadians, though stout, muscular fellows, were all so good-natured and phlegmatic in their faces that no danger of anything so desperate as an attack on their part was to be anticipated. It was decided, however, while they were on deck, to keep them confined to the forward part of the schooner.

This Zac succeeded in making known to them.

"We won't do you no harm," said he. "We won't tie you or bind you. At night you must go below to sleep. If any of you make an attack, we won't show you any mercy. So you'd best keep quiet."

The chief Acadian understood this as well by the signs with which it was accompanied as from the words, and he explained it to his followers. He then informed Zac that they would be quiet; whereupon Terry went forward and shook hands with each and all of them. "*Commy porty-voo? Bon jure, moo-soo,*" said he; to which the Acadians, however, made no response. They did indeed allow him to shake their hands; but they would not say anything, and evidently regarded him as a perjured villain, and traitor to their cause.

"Biler!" roared Zac. "Whar are you, you young cuss of life?"

Upon this the young cuss of life slowly emerged from the forecastle, holding a cold potato in his hand. The scene on deck made no impression on him, but he walked aft with his eyes fixed on Zac.

"Stand there!" commanded Zac; and Biler stood.

"Feller seamen and comrades at arms," said Zac, stretching out his arm in the oratorical fashion which he had seen used at town meetings "to hum." "This is a gellorious day for his great and gracious majesty King George, whose loyal subjects we air, as we have proved by this rescoo of his ship from the hands of the Philistines. It air all very well for the king to send out his red-coats; but I tell you what it is, I ain't seen a red-coat that lives that's equal to the natyve pro-vincial. Who air the ones that doos the best fightin' out here? The pro-vincials! Who air the men that's druv the wild and bloodthusty Injin back to his natyve woods? The pro-vincial! And who air the men that's goin' to settle the business of Moosoo, an' make America too hot to hold him an' his'n? The red-coats? Nay; but rayther the pro-vincials, the men that's fit the catamounts, an' bars, an' Injins, an' turned the waste an' howlin' wilderness into a gardin', an' made the desert blossom like a rose. So, I say, Hooray for the pro-vincials!"

At this Zac removed his hat. Terry did the same; so did Jericho. Biler had none to remove, but he raised his potato in the air. Zac led off — "Hip, hip, hip, h-o-o-o-r-a-a-a-y!"

"Arrah, captain, darlint, an' while ye's about it, sure ye won't be forgettin' ould Ireland," cried Terry, as the ringing cheers died away over the waters.

"Certingly," said Zac. "Course. Here goes!"

And three cheers in the same fashion followed for Terry's native land.

"Tare an' ages!" cried Terry; "an' while we're about it, sure an' we's ought to give three chairs for Africa, in honor of Jericho."

"Hooray!" cried Zac. "Here goes!" And three cheers followed for Africa. Whether Jericho knew much about Africa, may be a question; but he understood at least that this honor was offered to himself, and accepted it accordingly. It almost overwhelmed him. A wild chuckle of spasmodic delight burst from him, which threatened to end in a convulsion. And though he rallied from this, yet he was quite demoralized, and it was a long time before he settled down into that sedate old darky which was his normal condition.

And now Zac waited. Finding himself in command of his own schooner again, he felt more able to act in case of necessity. He was so far out from the shore that he was easily able to guard against the unexpected arrival of any boat. By day he lay at anchor; but when night came the Acadians were sent below, the anchor was raised, and the schooner cruised about the bay. The strong tides and currents caused a little trouble, but Zac soon got the run of them, at least in a general way, and several nights were thus passed. At length he began to grow impatient, and felt quite at a loss what to do. He was half inclined to send one of the Acadians ashore with a message, but as yet concluded to wait a little longer.

The Acadians, whether from fear or policy, did as they promised, and kept quiet. They kept by themselves always, and refused to accept the advances of

Terry, though they were frequently made. They all appeared listless and dejected, and the smiles, the laughter, and the singing which had characterized their first days on board had all passed away, and given place to low, murmured conversation or silence.

At length, one evening at about six o'clock, Zac saw a solitary boat coming from the shore. It was a long way off when he first saw it, and it seemed to be coming towards the schooner. The tide was unfavorable, so that the progress was quite slow; but its course lay steadily towards him, and Zac, who watched it intently, was turning over in his mind his best plan of action. It did not seem large enough to contain any very formidable force; but Zac thought best to take every precaution, and so sent all the Acadians below, while Terry and Jericho stood ready for action.

The time passed away, and the boat drew steadily nearer. At length it came near enough for Zac to see that it was rowed by two men, which sight was most welcome, since it assured him that no danger was to be apprehended. As he watched it, the boat drew nearer and nearer. He said nothing, but waited for them to speak first. He could see that both of the men were unarmed.

At last the boat touched the schooner's side. One of the men leaped on board, securing the boat, and the other followed immediately. They were both dressed like all the Acadians, but the second boatman had a slouched hat, which concealed his face. Zac, who carelessly regarded him, noticed that he was a smooth-faced boy, while the first boatman was a grizzled old man.

Both of these looked around, and seemed surprised. At length the boy advanced towards Zac.

"Capitaine," said this boy, "what ees dees? You no seem a preesonaire. You haf a gun. Air you free?"

At the sound of this voice Zac started back a step or two in utter amazement. Could it be possible? Yet that voice could not belong to any other. It must be. And even as he stood thus bewildered, the boy raised his hat with a shy smile, with which there was also much sadness mingled, and revealed the face of the little Margot.

"Wal," exclaimed Zac, "this does beat creation!"

Zac then caught both her hands, and held them in a tight grip, and for a few moments could not speak.

"I do feel good, little one," said he, in a tremulous voice. "This here's what I ben a waitin' for — to see you — an' you only — though I skurse dared to hope it. At any rate, I did hope and feel that you wouldn't go off without a word, and no more you heven't; an' I feel so happy that I could cry."

It was not exaggerated. Honest Zac was unused to such emotions, and hardly understood them. His eyes were moist as he looked upon Margot, and she saw that his simple confession was true. Her own emotion was as great as his. Tears started to her own eyes, and in her sadness she leaned on his arm and wept. Whereupon Zac's tears fell in spite of him, and he began to call himself a darned fool, and her a dear little pet; till the scolding of himself and the soothing of Margot became so hopelessly intermingled that he called her a darned old pet, and himself a dear little fool. Whereupon Margot burst into a laugh, dashed her tears away, and started off from Zac's grasp.

And now Margot proceeded to tell Zac the reason of her journey. From her he learned for the first time the events that had taken place on shore. First, she informed him that Claude was in confinement, and that Cazeneau intended to take him or send him to Louisbourg; that Cazeneau himself was bitterly hostile to him. She informed him that Laborde was dead; that Mimi was in terrible distress, and in mortal terror of Cazeneau; and finally, that she was to be taken to Louisbourg. All this filled Zac with concern and apprehension. She informed Zac that she and her mistress were to be taken away early on the following morning, and that she had slipped off thus in disguise, with the consent of her mistress, to let him know the danger of his friend; for Claude was to remain in Grand Pré for some time longer, and her mistress thought that after Cazeneau had departed, it might be possible to do something to save him.

This occupied some time, and Zac interrupted her with many questions. At length, having told her story, Margot turned away. This startled Zac.

"What!" said he; "you're not a goin' to leave me!" and poor Zac's voice was like a wail of despair.

"Why, what ees eet posseeble to do? I moos go to ma maitresse."

"But — but what'll become of me?" mourned Zac. "I may never see you again."

Margot sighed. "I moos go to ma maitresse," she murmured.

"O, don't! don't now!" cried Zac. "She ain't half

as fond of you as me. She can take care of herself. The priest'll watch over her. O, don't go, don't! I declar I feel like droundin' myself at the bare idee."

Zac, upon this, seized her hand, and begged, and coaxed, and prayed her to stay; till poor little Margot began to cry bitterly, and could only plead in broken tones her love for her dear mistress, who was in such danger, and how base it would be to desert her at such a time.

"Wal, wal — would you — would you come with me if — if it warn't for her?" mourned Zac.

Margot looked up at his face with a slight smile shining through her tears, which seemed to reassure poor Zac.

"We sall meet again," said Margot, in a more cheerful voice.

Zac shook his head disconsolately.

"And so, adieu," said Margot, in a low voice.

Zac said nothing, but with an expression of despair he took her in his arms, kissed her, and then turned away and wept.

Margot cried bitterly, and got into the boat. The old Acadian followed. The boat rowed away.

"*Adieu, et au revoir, cher Zac,*" said Margot, calling back and waving her hat.

"Goo-oo-d by-ye," said Zac, in a wail of despair.

For hours Zac stood looking after the boat in perfect silence. At last he turned away, gulping down a sigh.

"Darned ef I know what on airth's the matter with me," he murmured.

CHAPTER XIV.

MANŒUVRES OF ZAC.

ZAC slept but little that night. There were two causes for wakefulness. The first was Margot, who had wrought such mischief with his thoughts and feelings that he did not know what was the matter with him. The second cause was the condition of Claude.

Gradually Margot's image faded away, and he began to turn his thoughts towards the problem of delivering Claude. How was that to be done?

Over this he thought for the greater part of that night. Towards morning he called Terry, who was to watch for the remainder of the night, and proceeded to hold a council of war.

First of all he acquainted Terry with the general state of affairs. Part of Margot's information had been overheard by him; but Terry, seeing how things were, had discreetly withdrawn aft, and kept up a loud whistle, so as to prevent himself from overhearing their words; so that now the greater part of this information was news to the Irish boy.

"And have ye thought of anythin' at all, at all?" he asked.

"Wal, I've thought over most everythin'," said Zac. "You see, the state of the case is this: they've got one of us a prisoner ashore over there, but we've got six of them a prisoner out here."

"Thrue for you," said Terry.

"Wal, now, you see, if this Cazeneau was here, he hates Motier so like pison that he'd sacrifice a hundred Frenchmen rayther'n let him go — an' in my 'pinion he's worth a hundred Frenchmen, an' more. But now, bein' as Cazeneau's goin' away to-morrer, we'll be in a position to deal with the people here that's a keepin' Motier; an' when it comes to them — why, they won't feel like losin' six of their men for the sake of one stranger."

"I wonder," said Terry, "whether the owld boy that came out in the boat found out anythin'. 'Deed, if he'd had his wits about him, an' eyes in his head, he'd have seen it all, — so he would."

"Wal, we'll hev to let 'em know, right straight off."

"To-morra'd be best."

"Yes; an' then Cazeneau'll be off. I'd rayther wait till then; it'll be better for us to have him out of the way."

"What'll ye do?"

"Wal, I'll sail up, and send word ashore."

"How'll you sind word? We can't spake a word of the lingo."

"Wal, I ben a thinkin' it over, an' I've about come to the conclusion that the old Frenchman down thar in the cabin'll be the best one to send."

"Sure, an' ye won't sind the Frenchman ashore in yer own boat!"

"Why not?"

"He'll niver bring it back; so he won't."

"Then we'll keep the other five Frenchmen."

"Sure, an' it's a hard thing altogether, so it is, to hev to thrust him. He'll be after rousin' the country, an' they'll power down upon us in five hundred fishin' boats; so they will."

"Wal, if I staid here to anchor, that might be dangerous," said Zac; "but I ain't got no idee of standin' still in one place for them to attack me."

"Sure, an' it'll be best to let him see that if he don't come back wid Misther Motier, the whole five'll hev their brains blown out."

"Sartin. He'll have to go with that in his mind; an' what's more, I'll make him swear an oath to come back."

"Sure, an' it'll be the hard thing to do when neither of yez ondherstan' enough of one another's lingo to ax the time af day."

"Wal, then I'll have to be satisfied with the other five Moosoos. If the first Moosoo runs for it, he'll leave the other five, an' I ain't goin' to b'lieve that the farmers here air goin' to let five of their own relatives and connections perish, rayther'n give up one stranger."

A few more words followed, and then Zac retired below, leaving Terry on deck.

A few hours' sleep sufficed for Zac, and not long after sunrise he was all ready for action. But the tide was not quite high enough for his purposes. The long-extended mud flats lay bare in the distance for miles, and Zac had to wait until a portion, at least, of this space should be covered. At length the water had spread over as much of the red mud as seemed desirable, while every hour the schooner would have a greater depth beneath her; so Zac concluded to start. Up then went the anchor, the sails were set, and yielding to the impulse of a favorable breeze, the Parson turned her head towards the landing-place at Grand Pré.

Various preparations had to be made, and these now engaged the attention of Zac, who committed the care of the helm to Terry. The first was the composition of a letter. It was to be short and to the point. Zac had already settled in his own mind about the wording of this, so that the writing of it now occupied but a little time. It was as follows:—

"*To any Magistrate at Grand Pré:—*

"Know all men by this, that the six Acadians sent to take charge of the schooner 'Rev. Amos Adams,' are now held by me as my prisoners until such time as Mr. Claude Motier shall be delivered free from prison. And if Mr. Claude Motier shall not be set free, these six shall be carried to prison to Boston. And if Mr. Claude Motier be put to death, these six shall one and all be put to death likewise.

"An answer is required within three hours.
                    "Zion Awake Cox,
        "Master of the schooner 'Rev. Amos Adams.'
"Minas Basin, May 28, 1743."

This Zac folded and addressed, thinking that if no one in Grand Pré could read English, it would be taken to Claude himself for translation.

He next prepared to hoist a large British ensign. It was not often that the Parson showed her colors, but on this occasion it was necessary, and Zac saw that this display of English colors would be an act which would tell its own story, and show Moosoo that the schooner had once more changed masters. The colors lay on deck, ready to be hoisted at the proper moment. What that moment was to be he had already decided. Zac, in his preparations on this occasion, showed that he possessed a fine eye for dramatic effect, and knew how to create a sensation. There was a small howitzer amidships, — Zac's joy and pride, — which, like the ensign, was made use of only on great and rare occasions, such as the king's birthday, or other seasons of general rejoicing. This he determined to make use of at the present crisis, thinking that it would speak in tones that would strike terror to the heart of Moosoo, both on board and ashore.

Last of all, it remained to explain to the Acadians on board the purposes upon which he was bent. They were still below. Jericho had supplied them with their breakfast there, but Zac had not allowed them on deck. Now, however, he summoned forth their chief man, leaving the others behind, and proceeded to endeavor, as far as possible, to explain to this man what he wished.

The Acadian's stock of English words was but small, yet Zac was able, after all, by the help of signs, to give him some idea of his purpose. The letter also was shown him, and he seemed able to gather from it a general idea of its meaning. His words to Zac indicated a very lively idea of the danger which was impending over the prisoners.

"Me go," he said. "Put me 'shore. Me go *tout de suite;* me deliver M. Motier; make come here *tout de suite — bon!*"

"All right," said Zac; "but mind you, he must be

here in three hours — three," he repeated, holding up three fingers; "three hours."

"O, *oui* — yes — *certainement* — tree hour."

"These others will be all prisoners if he don't come."

"O, *oui* — yes; all personaire; *mais* he vill come, *tout certainement.*"

"You und'stand now, Moosoo, sure?"

"O, *oui;* me *comprends* — ond'stand — *certainement.*"

"Well, then, you wait up here till we get nearer, and then you can go ashore in the boat."

But Zac's preparations were destined to undergo some delay, for the wind died out, and the schooner lay idle upon the surface of the water. For several hours Zac waited patiently, hoping for a change; but no change came. At length the tide turned, and after a time the schooner, which had already been drifting helplessly, now began to be carried back towards the place from which she had started.

Zac was now left to his own invention, and could only decide that on the following day, if the wind should fail him, he would send the boat ashore from his present anchorage, and wait the result. For various reasons, however, he preferred going nearer; and therefore he had refrained from sending the boat ashore that day.

The next day came. There was a fresh breeze and a favorable one. The waters began to rise. Zac was all ready. Up went the anchor, the sails were set, and once more the Parson was turned towards the landing. The breeze now blew steadily, and in course of time Zac found himself sufficiently near for his purposes, and he began to act.

First of all, up went the British ensign. Then, the howitzer was fired. The noise of the report did not fail of the effect which Zac had anticipated. He saw the people turning out from their houses, some standing still and looking, others running towards the landing. Again and again the gun was fired, each report serving to increase the excitement among the people ashore. The British ensign was fully visible, and showed them what had taken place.

After this Zac sent Jericho ashore in the boat, along with the chief Acadian. The others were confined below. Zac saw the Acadian land, and Jericho return. Then he waited.

But it was not possible for him to wait here, nor was it safe. The tide would soon fall, leaving, as it retreated, a vast expanse of bare mud flats. He did not wish to run any risk of the schooner grounding in a place like this, and therefore allowed her to fall with the tide, and gradually move back to the bay without. All the time, however, he kept one eye on the shore. The three hours passed. He had drifted down again for several miles, and it was no longer easy to discern objects. But at length he saw a boat sailing from the shore to the schooner.

As the boat came nearer, he saw that Claude was not on board. Two men were in her, one of whom was the man whom he had sent away, and the other was a stranger. This stranger was an elderly man, of venerable appearance. They came up, and both went on board.

The elderly man was one of the chief men of the settlement, and spoke English sufficiently well to carry on a conversation. The information which he gave Zac was not at all to the satisfaction of the latter. It was to the following effect: —

That M. Motier had been kept in confinement at the house of Comeau; that early on the previous day M. Cazeneau had departed for Louisbourg, with the Abbé Michel, and the Countess de Laborde and her maid; that M. Motier, however, on the previous night, had somehow effected his escape.

Then the old man tried to induce Zac to set the Acadians free, except one, arguing that one life was enough to hold against that of Motier. But to this Zac sternly responded that one hundred Acadians would not be of sufficient value to counterbalance the sacred life of his friend. The only thing that Zac conceded was the liberty of the Acadian whom he had sent ashore; for he felt touched by the plucky conduct of this man in returning to the schooner. To his amazement, however, this man refused to go, declaring that he had come back to stand by his friends, and one of the others might be freed instead. On referring the matter to them, one was found who was weak enough to take advantage of this offer, and he it was who rowed the old man ashore.

Towards evening a canoe came gliding over the water, containing a single Indian. This Indian held aloof at a certain distance, scanning the schooner curiously. Zac, seeing this, sprang upon the taffrail, and called and beckoned to him; for a sudden thought came to him that the Indian might have been despatched by Claude to tell him something, and not knowing that he was no longer a prisoner, might be hesitating as to the best way of approaching. His conjecture seemed to be right, for this Indian, on seeing him, at once drew near, and came on board.

The Indian said not a word, but handed Zac a letter. Zac opened it, and read the following : —

" Claude Motier is free. Indians hafe safed him, and guide him to Louisbourg on the trail of Cazeneau. He wishes that you go to Canso, where you will be useful. He hope to safe Comtesse de Laborde, and want you to help to safe she. Go, then, to Canso; and if you arrive immediately, you sall see Indians, and must tell. They sall bing the intelligence to us.
"THE PERE MICHEL."

On reading this, Zac understood all. He saw that Père Michel had been a friend, and had engaged the Indians to help Claude. He at once determined to go to Canso. That very night he sent the Acadians ashore, and set sail.

CHAPTER XV.

FLIGHT.

ON leaving the house, the Indian led the way in silence for some distance. In the immediate neighborhood of the house were open fields, while in front of it was the road which ran down to the river. The house was on the declivity of a hill, at the foot of which were broad dike-lands, which ran far out till they terminated at the island already mentioned. Beyond this lay the Basin of Minas, and in the distance the shadowy outline of the surrounding shores.

The Indian led the way for some distance across the fields, and then turned into the road. Along this he passed till he reached the river. It was the Gaspereaux, at the mouth of which was the place where Claude had landed. Here the Indian crossed, and Claude followed, the water not being much above their knees. On reaching the other side, the Indian walked down the stream, keeping in the open as much as possible.

At length they left the river, and went on where the ground rose gradually. Here they soon entered the woods. It was a broad trail, and though in the shadow of the trees it was rather dark, yet the trail was wide enough to allow of Claude following his guide without any difficulty whatever. For about an hour they walked on in this way, ascending steadily most of the time, until at length Claude found himself upon an open space overgrown with shrubbery, and altogether bare of trees. Here several dusky figures appeared, and the guide conversed with them for some time.

Claude now seated himself on the ground. He felt so fatigued already from this first tramp, that he began to experience a sense of discouragement, and to think that his confinement had affected his strength. He gazed wearily and dreamily upon the scene before him. There, spread out at his feet, was a magnificent prospect. The land went sloping down to the water. Towards the left were the low dike-lands running out to the island; beyond this the waters of Minas Basin lay spread out before him. Thus far there had been no moonlight; but now, as he looked towards the east, he noticed that the sky was already flushing with the tints of dawn. But even this failed to rouse him. A profound weariness and inertness settled slowly over every sense and limb, and falling back, he fell into a deep sleep.

When he awaked, he saw that it was broad day, and that the sun was already high up in the sky. He started to his feet, and his first thought was one of joy at finding that his strength had all returned.

At his question, the Indian who was the spokesman told him that Louisbourg was more than twelve days' journey away, and that the path lay through the woods for the whole distance.

Before setting forth, the Indian gave him a rifle and a sword, which he said Père Michel had requested him to give him. There was also a sufficient supply of powder and ball. Taking these, Claude then set out on his long tramp. There were six Indians. Of these, three went in front, and three in the rear, the whole party going in single file. The trail was a wide one, and comparatively smooth. The guide drew Claude's attention to tracks on the ground, which could easily be recognized as the prints of horse hoofs. To Claude's inquiry how many there were, the Indian informed him that there were four. By this it seemed to Claude that Mimi and her maid had each one, while the other two were used by Cazeneau and the priest.

After several hours they at length came to a river. It was like the Gaspereaux in one respect, for it was turbid, and rolled with a swift current. The banks also were lined with marshes, and the edges were composed of soft mud. No way of crossing it appeared, and as they approached it, the Indians turned away to go up the stream. The prospect of a long *détour* was very unpleasant to Claude; and when at length he came to a place where the tracks of the horses went towards the river, he asked why this was. The Indians informed him that the horses had crossed here, but that they would have to go farther up. It did not turn out so bad as Claude had feared, for after about half an hour's further walk, they stopped at the bank of the river, and waited.

To Claude's question why they waited, an extraordinary answer was given. It was, that they were waiting till the water ran out. This reminded him of the old classic story about the fool who came to a river bank and waited for the water to run out, so that he might cross. Claude could not understand it; but, supposing that his guides knew what they were about, he waited for the result, taking advantage of this rest to fortify his inner man with a sound repast. After this was over, he rose to examine the situation; and the first sight showed him an astonishing change. He had lingered over his repast, now eating, now smoking, for about an hour, and in that time there had been wrought what seemed to him like a wonder of Nature. The water of the river had indeed been running out, as the Indian said; and there before him lay the channel, running low, with its waters still pouring forward at a rate which seemed to threaten final emptiness. And as he looked, the waters fell lower and lower, until at length, after he had been there three hours, the channel was almost empty.

This particular spot was not so muddy as other parts of the river bed, and therefore it had been chosen as the best place for crossing. It was quite hard, except in the middle, where the mud and water together rose over their knees; and thus this mighty flood was crossed as though it had been some small brook.

A few hours more served to bring them to the foot of some hills; and here the party halted. They had once more picked up the trail, and Claude was encouraged by the sight of the horse tracks.

He now unfolded to the Indian his design. To his great pleasure he found that Père Michel had already anticipated him, and that the Indian understood very well what was wanted. He assured Claude that he could easily communicate with the others so as not to be suspected, and lead back Père Michel and the women to him. His plan was to make a *détour*, and get ahead of them, approaching them from that direction, so as to avoid suspicion, while Claude might remain with the other Indians in some place where they could be found again. This plan seemed to Claude so simple and so feasible that he grew exultant over the prospect, forgetting the many difficulties that would still be before him, even if this first enterprise should succeed.

Their repast was simple and easily procured. The woods and waters furnished all that they required. A hare and some snipe and plover, with a few trout and a salmon, were the result of a short excursion, that did not extend much farther than a stone's throw from the encampment.

The next day they resumed their journey. It lay over the hills, which were steep, though not very high. The trail now grew rougher, being covered with stones in many places, so as to resemble the dry channel of a mountain torrent, while in other places the roots of trees which ran across interfered with rapid progress. This Claude saw with great satisfaction, for he knew that horses could go but slowly over a path like this; and therefore every step seemed to lessen the distance between him and Mimi. All that day they were traversing these hills.

The next day their journey lay through a gentle, undulating country, where the towering trees of the forest rose high all around, while at their feet were mosses, and wild grasses, and ferns, and flowers of a kind that were utterly strange to Claude. It was the month of June, the time when all nature in Acadie robes herself in her fairest charms.

Thus day after day passed, each day being the counterpart of the other in its cloudless skies, its breath from the perfumed woods, and the song of birds.

On the sixth day the tracks of the horses seemed to be fresher than usual; and to Claude's question the Indian replied that they must be close by them. At this Claude hurried on more vigorously, and kept up his march later than usual. He was even anxious to go forward all night; but the Indian was unwilling. He wished to approach them by day rather than by night, and was afraid of coming too suddenly upon them, and thus being discovered, if they went on while the others might be resting. Thus Claude was compelled to restrain his impatient desires, and wait for the following day.

When it came they set forth, and kept up a rapid pace for some hours. At length they came to an opening in the woods where the scene was no longer shut in by trees, but showed a wide-extended prospect. It was a valley, through which ran a small stream, bordered on each side with willows. The valley was green with the richest vegetation. Clusters of maples appeared like groves, here and there interspersed with beech and towering oaks, while at intervals appeared the magnificent forms of grand elms all covered with drooping foliage, and even the massive trunks green with the garlands of tender and gracefully-bending shoots.

For a moment Claude stood full of admiration at this lovely scene, and then hurried on after his guide. The guide now appeared desirous of slackening his pace, for he saw that if the other party were not far away he would be more liable to discovery in this open valley; but it was not very wide. About half a mile farther on, the deep woods arose once more; and, as there were no signs of life here, he yielded to Claude's impatient entreaty, and went on at his usual pace.

Half way across the valley there was a grove of maple trees; the path ran close beside it, skirting it, and then going beyond it. Along this they went, and were just emerging from its shelter, when the guide made a warning movement, and stood still. The next instant Claude was at his side. The Indian grasped Claude's arm, and made a stealthy movement backward.

That very instant Claude saw it all. A man was there — a European. Two Indians were with him. He was counting some birds which the Indians were carrying. It seemed as though they had been shooting through the valley, and this was their game. They could not have been shooting very recently, however, as no sound had been heard. This was the sight that met Claude's eyes as he stood by the Indian, and as the Indian grasped his arm.

It was too late. The European looked up. It was Cazeneau!

For a moment he stood staring at Claude as though he was some apparition. But the Indians who were behind, and who came forward, not knowing what was the matter, gave to this vision too practical a character; and Cazeneau saw plainly enough that, however unaccountable it might be, this was in very deed the man whom he believed to be in safe confinement at Grand Pré. A bitter curse escaped him. He rushed towards Claude, followed by his Indians.

"Scoundrel," he cried, "you have escaped! Aha! and do you dare to come on my track! This time I will make sure of you."

He gnashed his teeth in his fury, and, snatching a rifle from one of his Indians who were near him, aimed it at Claude, and pulled the trigger.

But the trigger clicked, and that was all. It was not loaded. With another curse Cazeneau dashed the rifle to the ground, and turned towards the other Indian. All this had been the work of a moment. The next moment Claude sprang forward with drawn sword.

"Villain," he cried, "and assassin! draw, and fight like a man!"

At these words Cazeneau was forced to turn, without having had time to get the other Indian's rifle, for Claude was close to him, and the glittering steel flashed before his eyes. He drew his sword, and retreating backward, put himself on guard.

"Seize this fellow!" he cried to his Indians; "seize him! In the name of your great father, the King of France, seize him, I tell you!"

The Indians looked forward. There, behind Claude, they saw six other Indians — their own friends. They shook their heads.

"Too many," said they.

"You fellows!" cried Cazeneau to Claude's Indians, "I am the officer of your great father, the King of France. This man is a traitor. I order you to seize him, in the king's name."

Claude's Indians stood there motionless. They did not seem to understand.

All this time Cazeneau was keeping up a defence, and parrying Claude's attack. He was a skilful swordsman, and he wished to take Claude alive if possible, rather than to fight with him. So he tried once more. He supposed that Claude's Indians did not understand. He therefore told his Indians to tell the others in their language what was wanted. At this the two walked over to the six, and began talking.

Caseneau watched them earnestly. He saw, to his infinite rage, that his words had no effect whatever on Claude's Indians.

"Coward," cried Claude, "coward and villain! you must fight. My Indians are faithful to me. You hate to fight, — you are afraid, — but you must, or I will beat you to death with the blade of my sword."

At this Cazeneau turned purple with rage. He saw how it was. He determined to show this colonist all his skill, and wound him, and still take him alive. So, with a curse, he rushed upon Claude. But his own excitement interfered with that display of skill which he intended to show; and Claude, who had regained his coolness, had the advantage in this respect.

A few strokes showed Cazeneau that he had found his master. But this discovery only added to his rage. He determined to bring the contest to a speedy issue. With this intent he lunged forward with a deadly thrust. But the thrust was turned aside, and the next instant Claude's sword passed through the body of Cazeneau.

CHAPTER XVI.

REUNION.

THE wounded man fell to the ground, and Claude, dropping his sword, sank on his knees beside him. In that one instant all his anger and his hate fled away. It was no longer Cazeneau, his mortal enemy, whom he saw, but his fellow-creature, laid low by his hand. The thought sent a quiver through every nerve, and it was with no ordinary emotion that Claude sought to relieve his fallen enemy. But Cazeneau was unchanged in his implacable hate; or, if possible, he was even more bitter and more malignant now, since he had thus been beaten.

"Away!" he cried, in a faint voice. "Away! Touch me not. Do not exult yet, Montresor. You think you have — avenged — your cursed father — and your mother. Do not exult too soon; at least you are — a pauper — a pauper — a pauper! Away! My own people — will care for me."

Claude rose at this, and motioned to Cazeneau's Indians. They came up. One of them examined the wound. He then looked up at Claude, and solemnly shook his head.

"May Heaven have mercy on his soul!" murmured Claude. "I thank Heaven that I do not know all the bitter wrong that he has done to my parents. What he has done to me I forgive."

Then, by a sudden impulse, he bent down over the fallen man. "Cazeneau," said he, "you're a dying man. You have something on your conscience now. What you have done to me I forgive. May others whom you have injured do the same."

At this magnanimous speech Cazeneau rolled his glaring eyes furiously towards the young man, and then, supplied with a sudden spasmodic strength by his own passion, he cried out, with bitter oaths and execrations, —

"Curse you! you and all your race!"

He raised himself slightly as he said this. The next instant he fell back, senseless. For a moment Claude stood looking at the lifeless form, undecided what to do. Should he remain here longer? If Cazeneau should revive, it would only be to curse him; if he died, he could do nothing. Would it not be better to hurry forward after the rest of the party, who could not be very far away? If so, he could send back the priest, who would come in time either for life or death. The moment that he thought of this he decided that he would hurry forward for the priest. He then explained to his guide what he wished, and asked the Indians of Cazeneau how far the rest of the party were. They could speak but very little French, but managed to make Claude understand that they were not far. To his Indian they said more, and he told his employer. What they said was to this effect: that on this morning Cazeneau had left the party with these two Indians, for the sake of a little recreation in hunting. The rest had gone forward, with the understanding that they should not go more than two or three hours. Then they were to halt and wait. Cazeneau was just about to go after them as Claude came up.

"Curse you and all your Race." Page 164.

This information showed Claude that the rest of the party were within easy distance, and that the priest could be reached and sent back before evening. Accordingly he hesitated no longer, but set forth at once in the greatest haste.

The thought that Mimi was so near inspired Claude with fresh energy. Although he had been on the tramp all day, and without rest, — although he had received a severe and unparalleled shock in the terrible fate of Cazeneau, — yet the thought of Mimi had sufficient power over him to chase away the gloom that for a time had fallen over his soul. It was enough to him now that a priest was within reach. Upon that priest he could throw all the responsibility which arose out of the situation of his enemy. These were the thoughts that animated him, and urged him forward.

The Indians of Cazeneau had made him understand that they were only a few hours ahead; but Claude thought that they were even nearer. He thought it unlikely that Cazeneau would let them go very far, and supposed that he had ordered the other Indians to go slowly, and halt after about three or four miles. He therefore confidently expected to come up with them after traversing about that distance.

With this belief he urged on his attendants, and himself put forth all his powers, until at length, after nearly two hours, he was compelled to slacken his speed. This showed that they were not so near as he had expected; yet still he believed that they were just ahead, and that he would come up with them every moment.

Thus his mind was kept upon a constant strain, and he was always on the lookout, watching both with eyes and ears either to see some sign of them, or to hear them as they went on before him. And this constant strain of mind and of sense, and this sustained attitude of expectation, made the way seem less, and the time seem short; and thus, though there was a certain disappointment, yet still the hope of seeing them every next minute kept up his spirits and his energies. Thus he went on, like one who pursues an *ignis fatuus*, until at length the light of day faded out, and the shades of night settled down over the forest.

He would certainly have thought that he had missed the way, had it not been for one fact; and that was, that the track of the party whom he was pursuing was as plain as ever, and quite fresh, showing that they had passed over it this very day. The Indians with him were all certain of this. It showed him that however fast he had gone, they had been going yet faster, and that all his eagerness to catch up with them had not been greater than their eagerness to advance. Why was this? Suddenly the whole truth flashed upon his mind.

The priest had unexpectedly shaken off Cazeneau. He had evidently resolved to try to escape. His strange influence over the Indians had, no doubt, enabled him to make them his accomplices. With the hope, therefore, of shaking off Cazeneau, he had hurried on as fast as possible.

Still there was one thing, and that was, that they would have to bring up somewhere. It was more than probable that the priest would try to reach Canso. In that case Claude had only to keep on his track, and he would get to that place not very long after him; sufficiently soon, at any rate, to prevent missing him. As to Louisbourg, if the priest should go there, he also could go there, and with impunity now, since his enemy was no more. As for the unhappy Cazeneau, he found himself no longer able to send him the priest; but he did not feel himself to blame for that, and could only hope that he might reach the priest before it should be altogether too late.

A slight repast that night, which was made from some fragments which he had carried in his pocket, a few hours' sleep, and another slight repast on the following morning, made from an early bird which he had shot when it was on its way to get its worm, served to prepare him for the journey before him.

The Indians informed him that the Strait of Canso was now not more than a day and a half distant. The news was most welcome to Claude. The Strait of Canso seemed like a place where the priest would be compelled to make some sort of a halt, either while waiting for a chance to cross or while making a *détour* to get to Canso. For his part, he would have one great advantage, and that was, that he would not be compelled to think about his course. All that he had to do was to follow the track before him as rapidly and as perseveringly as possible.

All that day Claude hurried onward without stopping to halt, being sustained by his own burning impatience, and also by that same hope which had supported him on the preceding day. But it was, as before, like the pursuit of an *ignis fatuus*, and ever the objects of his pursuit seemed to elude him.

At length, towards the close of the day, they reached a river, and the trail ran along by its side for miles, sometimes leaving it, and again returning to it. The path was broad, the woods were free from underbrush, and more open than usual.

Suddenly the guide stopped and looked forward, with the instinct of his Indian caution. But Claude had one idea only in his mind, and knowing well that there could be no enemy now, since Cazeneau was out of the way, he hurried onward. Some moving figures attracted his gaze. Then he saw horses, and some men and women. Then he emerged from the trees, bursting forth at a run into an open place which lay upon the river bank. One glance was sufficient. It was the priest and his party. With a cry of joy he rushed forward. The others saw him coming. The priest turned in amazement; for he had no idea that Claude was so near. Before he could speak a word, however, the young man had flung himself into his arms, and the priest returned his embrace with equal warmth. Claude then turned to Mimi, who was standing near, and in the rapture of that meeting was on the point of catching her in his arms also; but Mimi saw the movement, and retreated shyly, while a mantling blush over her lovely features showed both joy and confusion. So Claude had to content himself with taking her hand, which he seized in both of his, and held as though he would never let go.

After these first greetings, there followed a torrent of questions from both sides. The priest's story was but a short one. On the day when Cazeneau had left them, he had gone on a short hunting excursion, simply for the sake of relieving the monotony of the long tramp. He had charged the Indians not to go farther than two hours ahead. His intention was to make a circuit, and join them by evening. But the Indians were altogether under the influence of Père Michel, and were willing to do anything that he wished. The "Great Father,"— the French king,— with whom Cazeneau thought he could overawe them, was in truth a very shadowy and unsubstantial personage. But Père Michel was one whom they knew, and for some reason regarded with boundless veneration. When, therefore, he proposed to them to go on, they at once acceded. For Père Michel caught at this unexpected opportunity to escape, which was thus presented, and at once set forth at the utmost possible speed. He travelled all that day and far into the night, until he thought that a sufficient distance had been put between himself and Cazeneau to prevent capture. He would have gone much farther on this day had it not been for Mimi, who, already fatigued by her long journey, was unable to endure this increased exertion, and after trying in vain to keep up, was compelled to rest. They had been encamping here for about three hours, and were already deliberating about a night journey, when Claude came up.

The time had been spent in constructing a sort of litter, which the priest intended to sling between two horses, hoping by this means to take Mimi onward with less fatigue. He had made up his mind, as Claude indeed had suspected, to make for Canso, so as to put himself out of the reach of Cazeneau.

Claude then told the priest his story, to which the latter listened with deep emotion. He had not anticipated anything like this. Amazed as he had been at the sudden appearance of Claude, he had thought that by some happy accident the young man had eluded Cazeneau, and he now learned how it really was.

For some time he said not a single word, and indeed there was nothing that he could say. He knew well that Claude had been deeply and foully wronged by Cazeneau, and he knew also that this last act was hardly to be considered as anything else than the act of Cazeneau himself, who first attacked Claude, and forced him to fight.

But there still remained to be considered what might now be done. Claude's first thought was the one which had been in his mind during the past day; that is to say, he still thought of sending the priest back to Cazeneau, without thinking of the distance, and the time that now lay between. His excitement had prevented him from taking this into consideration. The priest, however, at once reminded him of it.

"I do not see," said he, "what I can do. You forget how long it is since you left him. He must be dead and buried by this time. Even if he should linger longer than you expected, I could not hope to reach that place in time to do anything, not even to bury him. It is a good two days' journey from here to there. It is two days since you left him. It would take two days more for me to reach him. That makes four days. By that time, if he is dead, he would already be buried; and if he is living, he would be conveyed by the Indians to some place of rest and shelter.

"As long as I thought that Cazeneau was pursuing us," continued the priest, "I tried to advance as rapidly as possible, and intended to go to Canso, where I should be safe from him. But now that he can trouble us no more, there is no reason why we should not go to Louisbourg. That will be better for Mimi, and it will also suit my views better. You, too, may as well go there, since you will be able to carry out your own plans, whatever they are, from that place better than from any other."

The result of this conversation was, that they decided to go to Louisbourg.

CHAPTER XVII.

AMONG FRIENDS.

IN order to make their escape the more certain, the priest had carried off the horse which Cazeneau had used, so that now Claude was no more obliged to go on foot. Mimi no longer complained of fatigue, but was able to bear up with the fatigues of the rest of the journey in a wonderful way. Claude did not seem inclined to make much use of the spare horse, for he walked much of the way at Mimi's side, and where there was not room, he walked at her horse's head.

The remainder of the journey occupied about four days, and it was very much like what it had been; that is, a track through the woods, sometimes rough, sometimes smooth. The whole track showed marks of constant use, which the priest explained to Claude as being caused by droves of cattle, which were constantly being sent from Grand Pré to Louisbourg, where they fetched a handsome price. The Indian trails in other places were far rougher and narrower, besides being interrupted by fallen trees. The only difficulty that they had to encounter was in crossing the Strait of Canso; but after following the shore for a few miles, they came to a place where there was a barge, used to transport cattle. Two or three French fishermen lived here, and they took the whole party over to the opposite side. After this they continued their journey.

That journey seemed to Claude altogether too short. Each day passed away too rapidly. Wandering by the side of Mimi through the fragrant forests, under the clear sky, listening to her gentle voice, and catching the sweet smile of her innocent face, it seemed to him as though he would like to go on this way forever. A cloud of sadness rested on her gentle brow, which made her somewhat unlike the sprightly girl of the schooner, and more like the despairing maid whom he had rescued on the raft.

But there was reason for this sadness. Mimi was a fond and loving daughter. She had chosen to follow her father across the ocean, when she might have lived at home in comfort; and the death of that father had been a terrible blow. For some time the blow had been alleviated by the terrors which she felt about Cazeneau and his designs. But now, since he and his designs were no more to be thought of, the sorrow of her bereavement returned.

Still, she was not without consolation, and even joy. It was joy to her to have escaped from the man and from the danger that she dreaded. It was also joy to her to find herself once more in company with Claude, in whom she had all along taken a tender interest. Until she heard his story from his own lips she had not had any idea that he had been the victim of Cazeneau. She had supposed that he was in the schooner all the time, and had wondered why he did not make his appearance. And her anxiety about her father, and grief over his death, prevented her from dwelling much upon this.

At length they came in sight of the sea. The trees here were small, stunted, and scrubby; the soil was poor, the grass coarse and interspersed with moss and stones. In many places it was boggy, while in others it was rocky. Their path ran along the shore for some miles, and then entered the woods. For some distance farther they went on, and then emerged into an open country, where they saw before them the goal of their long journey.

Open fields lay before them, with houses and barns. Farther on there lay a beautiful harbor, about five or six miles long and one mile wide, with a narrow entrance into the outer sea, and an island which commanded the entrance. Upon this island, and also on one side of the entrance, were batteries, while on the side of the harbor on which they were standing, and about two miles away, was another battery, larger than either of these. At the farthest end of the harbor were small houses of farmers or fishermen, with barns and cultivated fields. In the harbor were some schooners and small fishing vessels, and two large frigates.

But it was upon the end of the harbor nearest to themselves that their eyes turned with the most pleasure. Here Louisbourg stood, its walls and spires rising before them, and the flag of France floating from the citadel. The town was about half a mile long, surrounded by a stockade and occasional batteries. Upon the highest point the citadel stood, with the guns peeping over the parapet. The path here entered a road, which ran towards the town; and now, going to this road, they went on, and soon reached the gate.

On entering the gate, they were stopped and questioned; but the priest, who seemed to be known, easily satisfied his examiners, and they were allowed to go on. They went along a wide street, which, however, was unpaved, and lined on each side with houses of unpretending appearance. Most of them were built of wood, some of logs, one or two of stone. All were of small size, with small doors and windows, and huge, stumpy chimneys. The street was straight, and led to the citadel, in which was the governor's residence. Other streets crossed at right angles with much regularity. There were a few shops, but not many. Most of these were lower down, near the water, and were of that class to which the soldiers and sailors resorted. Outside the citadel was a large church, built of undressed stone, and without any pretensions to architectural beauty. Beyond this was the entrance to the citadel. This place was on the crest of the hill, and was surrounded by a dry ditch and a wall. A drawbridge led across the ditch to the gate. On reaching this place the party had to stop, and the priest sent in his name to the governor or commandant. After waiting some time, a message came to admit them. Thereupon they all passed through, and found themselves inside the citadel.

They found this to be an irregular space, about two hundred feet in length and width, surrounded by walls, under which were arched cells, that were used for storage or magazines, and might also serve as casemates in time of siege. There were barracks at one end, and at the other the governor's residence, built of stone. Upon the parade troops were exercising, and in front of the barracks a band was playing.

The whole scene was thus one of much animation; indeed, it seemed very much so to the eyes of these wanderers, so long accustomed to the solitude of the sea, or of the primeval forest. However, they did not wait to gaze upon the scene, but went on at once, without delay, to the commandant.

The commandant — Monsieur Auguste de Florian — received them with much politeness. He was a man of apparently about forty years of age, medium stature, and good-natured face, without any particular sign of character or talent in his general expression. This was the man whom Cazeneau was to succeed, whose arrival he had been expecting for a long time. He received the new comers politely, and, after having heard the priest's account of Mimi, — who she was, and how he had found her, — he at once sent for his wife, who took her to her own apartments, and informed her that this must be her home as long as she was at Louisbourg.

The commandant now questioned the priest more particularly about the Arethuse. Père Michel left the narration to Claude. He had been introduced under the name of M. Motier, and did not choose to say anything about his real name and rank, for fear that it might lead him into fresh difficulties. So Claude gave an account of the meeting between the schooner and the raft, and also told all that he knew about the fate of the Arethuse. The priest added something more that he had learned, and informed the commandant that he could learn all the rest from Mimi.

The governor's polite attention did not end with this visit. He at once set about procuring a place where Claude might stay, and would have done the same kind office to Père Michel, had not the priest declined. He had a place where he could stay with one of the priests of the town, who was a friend; and besides, he intended to carry on the duties of his sacred office. Claude, therefore, was compelled to separate himself from the good priest, who, however, assured him that he would see him often. Before evening he found himself in comfortable quarters in the house of the naval storekeeper, who received him with the utmost cordiality as the friend of the commandant.

The next day Claude saw Père Michel. He seemed troubled in mind, and, after some questions, informed him that he had come all the way to Louisbourg for the express purpose of getting some letters which he had been expecting from France. They should have been here by this time, but had not come, and he was afraid that they had been sent out in the Arethuse. If so, there might be endless trouble and confusion, since it would take too long altogether to write again and receive answers. It was a business of infinite importance to himself and to others; and Père Michel, who had never before, since Claude had known him, lost his serenity, now appeared quite broken down by disappointment.

His present purpose was to go back and see about the burial of Cazeneau; but he would wait for another week, partly for the sake of rest, and partly to wait until Cazeneau's Indians had been heard from. He had sent out two of the Indians who had come with him to make inquiries; and when they returned, he would go. He was also waiting in the hope that another ship might arrive. There was some talk of a frigate which was to bring out some sappers and engineers for the works. It was the Grand Monarque. She had not come as yet, nor had she left by last advices; but still she was liable to leave at any moment.

"Still," said the priest, "it is useless to expect anything or to hope for anything. The king is weak. He is nothing. How many years has he been a *roi fainéant?* Fleury was a fit minister for such a king. Weak, bigoted, conceited, Fleury had only one policy, and that was, to keep things quiet, and not suffer any change. If wrongs had been done, he refused to right them. Fleury has been a curse to France. But since his death his successors may be even worse. The state of France is hopeless. The country is overwhelmed with debt, and is in the hands of unprincipled vagabonds. The king has said that he would govern without ministers; but that only means that he will allow himself to be swayed by favorites. Fleury has gone, and in his place there comes — who? Why, the Duchesse de Chateauroux. She is now the minister of France."

The priest spoke with indescribable bitterness; so much so, indeed, that Claude was amazed.

"The latest news," continued Père Michel, "is, that England is going to send an army to assist Austria. The queen, Maria Theresa, will now be able to turn the scales against France. This means war, and the declaration must follow soon. Well, poor old Fleury kept out of war with England till he died. But that was Walpole's doing, perhaps. They were wonderful friends; and perhaps it was just as well. But this new ministry — this woman and her friends — they will make a change for France; and I only hope, while they are reversing Fleury's policy in some things, they'll do it in others.

"France," continued Père Michel, in a gloomy tone, "France is rotten to the core — all France, both at home and abroad. Why, even out here the fatal system reigns. This commandant," he went on, dropping his voice, "is as deeply implicated as any of them. He was appointed by a court favorite; so was Cazeneau. He came out with the intention of making his fortune, not for the sake of building up a French empire in America.

"It's no use. France can't build up an empire here. The English will get America. They come out as a people, and settle in the forest; but we come out as officials, to make money out of our country. Already the English are millions, and we are thousands. What chance is there for us? Some day an English army will come and drive us out of Ile Royale, and out of Canada, as they've already driven us out of Acadie. Our own people are discouraged; and, though they love France, yet they feel less oppressed under English rule. Can there be a worse commentary on French rule than that?

"And you, my son," continued the priest, in a milder tone, but one which was equally earnest, "don't think of going to France. You can do nothing there. It would require the expenditure of a fortune in bribery to get to the ears of those who surround the king; and then there would be no hope of obtaining justice from them. All are interested in letting things remain as they were. The wrong done was committed years ago. The estates have passed into other hands, and from one owner to another. The present holders are all-powerful at court; and if you were to go there, you would only wear out your youth, and accomplish nothing."

CHAPTER XVIII.

LOUISBOURG.

THERE was a little *beau monde* at Louisbourg, which, as might be expected, was quite gay, since it was French. At the head stood, of course, the commandant and his lady; then came the military officers with their ladies, and the naval officers without their ladies, together with the unmarried officers of both services. As the gentlemen far outnumbered the ladies, the latter were always in great demand; so that the ladies of the civilians, though of a decidedly inferior grade, were objects of attention and of homage. This being the case, it will readily be perceived what an effect was produced upon the *beau monde* at Louisbourg by the advent of such a bright, particular star as Mimi. Young, beautiful, accomplished, she also added the charms of rank, and title, and supposed wealth. The Count de Laborde had been prominent at court, and his name was well known. His daughter was therefore looked upon as one of the greatest heiresses of France, and there was not a young officer at Louisbourg who did not inwardly vow to strive to win so dazzling a prize.

She would at once have been compelled to undergo a round of the most exhaustive festivities, had it not been for one thing — she was in mourning. Her bereavement had been severe, and was so recent that all thoughts of gayety were out of the question. This fact lessened the chances which the gallant French cavaliers might otherwise have had, but in no respect lessened their devotion. Beauty in distress is always a touching and a resistless object to every chivalrous heart; and here the beauty was exquisite, and the distress was undeniably great.

The commandant and his lady had appropriated Mimi from the first, and Mimi congratulated herself on having found a home so easily. It was pleasant to her, after her recent imprisonment, to be among people who looked up to her with respectful and affectionate esteem. Monsieur de Florian may not have been one of the best of men; indeed, it was said that he had been diligently feathering his nest at the expense of the government ever since he had been in Louisbourg; but in spite of that, he was a kind-hearted man, while his wife was a kind-hearted woman, and one, too, who was full of tact and delicacy. Mimi's position, therefore, was as pleasant as it could be, under the circumstances.

After one or two days had passed, Claude began to be aware of the fact that life in Louisbourg was much less pleasant than life on the road. There he was all day long close beside Mimi, or at her horse's bridle, with confidential chat about a thousand things, with eloquent nothings, and shy glances, and tender little attentions, and delicate services. Here, however, it was all different. All this had come to an end. The difficulty now was, to see Mimi at all. It is true there was no lack of friendliness on the part of the commandant, or of his good lady; but then he was only one among many, who all were received with the same genial welcome by this genial and polished pair. The chivalry of Louisbourg crowded to do homage to the beautiful stranger, and the position of Claude did not seem to be at all more favorable than that of the youngest cadet in the service.

His obscurity now troubled Claude greatly. He found himself quite insignificant in Louisbourg. If he had possessed the smallest military rank, he would have been of more consequence. He thought of coming out in his true name, as the Count de Montresor, but was deterred by the thought of the troubles into which he had already fallen by the discovery of his name. How much of that arrest was due to the ill will of Cazeneau, and how much to the actual dangers besetting him as a Montresor, he could not know. He saw plainly enough that the declaration of his name and rank might lead to a new arrest at the hands of this commandant, in which case escape could hardly be thought of. He saw that it was better far for him to be insignificant, yet free, than to be the highest personage in Louisbourg, and liable to be flung into a dungeon. His ignorance of French affairs, and of the actual history of his family, made him cautious; so that he resolved not to mention the truth about himself to any one. Under all these circumstances, Claude saw no other resource but to endure as best he could the unpleasantness of his personal situation, and live in the hope that in the course of time some change might take place by which he could be brought into closer connection with Mimi.

Fortunately for him, an opportunity of seeing Mimi occurred before he had gone too deep down into despondency. He went up one day to the citadel, about a week after he had come to Louisbourg. Mimi was at the window, and as he came she saw him, and ran to the door. Her face was radiant with smiles.

"O, I am so glad," she said, "that you have come! I did so want to see you, to ask you about something!"

"I never see you alone now," said Claude, sadly, holding her hand as though unwilling to relinquish it.

"No," said Mimi, with a slight flush, gently withdrawing her hand, "I am never alone, and there are so many callers; but M. Florian has gone out, taking the madame, on an affair of some importance; and so, you see, we can talk without interruption."

"Especially if we walk over into the garden," said Claude.

Mimi assented, and the two walked into the garden that was on the west side of the residence, and for some time neither of them said a word. The trees had just come into leaf; for the season is late in this climate, but the delay is made good by the rapid growth of vegetation after it has once started; and now the leaves were bursting forth in glorious richness and profusion, some more advanced than others, and exhibiting every stage of development. The lilacs, above all, were conspicuous for beauty; for they were covered with blossoms, with the perfume of which the air was loaded.

"I never see you now," said Claude, at length.

"No," said Mimi, sadly.

"It is not as it used to be," said Claude, with a mournful smile, "when I walked by your side day after day."

Mimi sighed, and said nothing.

"It is different with you," said Claude; "you are the centre of universal admiration, and everybody pays you attention. The time never passes heavily with you; but think of me — miserable, obscure, friendless!"

Mimi turned, and looked at him with such a piteous face that Claude stopped short. Her eyes were fixed on his with tender melancholy and reproach. They were filled with tears.

"And do you really believe that?" she said — "that the time never passes heavily with me? It has been a sad time ever since I came here. Think how short a time it is since poor, dear papa left me! Do you think I can have the heart for much enjoyment?"

"Forgive me," said Claude, deeply moved; "I had forgotten; I did not think what I was saying; I was too selfish."

"That is true," said Mimi. "While you were suffering from loneliness, you should have thought that I, too, was suffering, even in the midst of the crowd. But what are they all to me? They are all strangers. It is my friends that I want to see; and you are away, and the good Père Michel never comes!"

"Were you lonely on the road?" asked Claude.

"Never," said Mimi, innocently, "after you came."

As she said this, a flush passed over her lovely face, and she looked away confused. Claude seized her hand, and pressed it to his lips. They then walked on in silence for some time. At last Claude spoke again.

"The ship will not leave for six weeks. If I were alone, I think I should go back to Boston. But if you go to France, I shall go, too. Have you ever thought of what you will do when you get there?"

"I suppose I shall have to go to France," said Mimi; "but why should you think of going to Boston? Are you not going on your family business?"

"I am not," said Claude. "I am only going because you are going. As to my family business, I have forgotten all about it; and, indeed, I very much doubt whether I could do anything at all. I do not even know how I am to begin. But I wish to see you safe and happy among your friends."

Mimi looked at him in sad surprise.

"I do not know whether I have any friends or not," said she. "I have only one relative, whom I have never seen. I had intended to go to her. I do not know what I shall do. If this aunt is willing to take me, I shall live with her; but she is not very rich, and I may be a burden."

"A burden!" said Claude; "that is impossible! And besides, such a great heiress as you will be welcome wherever you go."

He spoke this with a touch of bitterness in his voice; for Mimi's supposed possessions seemed to him to be the chief barrier between himself and her.

"A great heiress!" said Mimi, sadly. "I don't know what put that into your head. Unfortunately, as far as I know, I have nothing. My papa sold all his estates, and had all his money on board the Arethuse. It was all lost in the ship, and though I was an heiress when I left home, I shall go back nothing better than a beggar, to beg a home from my unknown aunt. Or," she continued, "if my aunt shows no affection, it is my intention to go back to the convent of St. Cecilia, where I was educated, and I know they will be glad to have me; and I could not find a better home for the rest of my life than among those dear sisters who love me so well."

"O, Mimi," he cried, "O, what joy it is to hear that you are a beggar! Mimi, Mimi! I have always felt that you were far above me — too far for me to raise my thoughts to you. Mimi, you are a beggar, and not an heiress! You must not go to France. I will not go. Let us remain together. I can be more to you than any friend. Come with me. Be mine. O, let me spend my life in trying to show you how I love you!"

He spoke these words quickly, feverishly, and passionately, seizing her hand in both of his. He had never called her before by her name; but now he called her by it over and over, with loving intonations. Mimi had hardly been prepared for this; but though unprepared, she was not offended. On the contrary, she looked up at him with a face that told him more than words could convey. He could not help reading its eloquent meaning. Her glance penetrated to his heart — her soul spoke to his. He caught her in his arms, and little Mimi leaned her head on his breast and wept.

But from this dream of hope and happiness they were destined to have a sudden and very rude awakening. There was a sound in the shrubbery behind them, and a voice said, in a low, cautious tone, —

"H-s-s-t!"

At this they both started, and turned. It was the Père Michel.

Both started as they saw him, partly from surprise, and partly, also, from the shock which they felt at the expression of his face. He was pale and agitated, and the calmness and self-control which usually characterized him had departed.

"My dear friend," said Claude, hurriedly, turning towards him and seizing his hand, "what is the matter? Are you not well? Has anything happened? You are agitated. What is the matter?"

"The very worst," said Père Michel — "M. de Cazeneau!"

"What of him? Why, he is dead!"

"Dead? No; he is alive. Worse — he is here — here — in Louisbourg. I have just seen him!"

"What!" cried Claude, starting back, "M. de Cazeneau alive, and here in Louisbourg! How is that possible?"

"I don't know," said the priest. "I only know this, that I have just seen him!"

"Seen him?"

"Yes."

"Where? You must be mistaken."

"No, no," said the priest, hurriedly. "I know him — only too well. I saw him at the Ordnance. He has just arrived. He was brought here by Indians, on a litter. The commandant is even now with him. I saw him go in. I hurried here, for I knew that you were here, to tell you to fly. Fly then, at once, and for your life. I can get you away now, if you fly at once."

"Fly?" repeated Claude, casting a glance at Mimi.

"Yes, fly!" cried the priest, in earnest tones. "Don't think of her, — or, rather, do you, Mimi, if you value his life, urge him, entreat him, pray him to fly. He is lost if he stays. One moment more may destroy him."

Mimi turned as pale as death. Her lips parted. She would have spoken, but could say nothing.

"Come," cried the priest, "come, hasten, fly! It may be only for a few weeks — a few weeks only — think of that. There is more at stake than you imagine. Boy, you know not what you are risking — not your own life, but the lives of others; the honor of your family; the hope of the final redemption of your race. Haste — fly, fly!"

The priest spoke in tones of feverish impetuosity. At these words Claude stood thunder-struck. It seemed as though this priest knew something about his family. What did he know? How could he allude to the honor of that family, and the hope of its redemption?

"O, fly! O, fly! Haste!" cried Mimi, who had at last found her voice. "Don't think of me. Fly — save yourself, before it's too late."

"What! and leave you at his mercy?" said Claude.

"O, don't think of me," cried Mimi; "save yourself."

"Haste — come," cried the priest; "it is already too late. You have wasted precious moments."

"I cannot," cried Claude, as he looked at Mimi, who stood in an attitude of despair.

"Then you are lost," groaned the priest, in a voice of bitterest grief.

Mimi suddenly caught Claude by the Arm. Page 189.

CHAPTER XIX.

THE CAPTIVE AND THE CAPTORS.

FURTHER conversation was now prevented by the approach of a company of soldiers, headed by the commandant. Mimi stood as if rooted to the spot, and then suddenly caught Claude by the arm, as though by her weak strength she could save him from the fate which was impending over him; but the priest interposed, and gently drew her away.

The soldiers halted at the entrance to the garden, and the commandant came forward. His face was clouded and somewhat stern, and every particle of his old friendliness seemed to have departed.

"I regret, monsieur," said he, "the unpleasant necessity which forces me to arrest you; but, had I known anything about your crime, you would have been put under arrest before you had enjoyed my hospitality."

"O, monsieur!" interrupted Mimi.

The commandant turned, and said, severely, "I trust that the Countess de Laborde will see the impropriety of her presence here. Monsieur L'Abbé, will you give the countess your arm into the house?"

Père Michel, at this, led Mimi away. One parting look she threw upon Claude, full of utter despair, and then, leaning upon the arm of the priest, walked slowly in.

Claude said not a word in reply to the address of the commandant. He knew too well that under present circumstances words would be utterly useless. If Cazeneau was indeed alive, and now in Louisbourg, then there could be no hope for himself. If the former charges which led to his arrest should be insufficient to condemn him, his attack upon Cazeneau would afford sufficient cause to his enemy to glut his vengeance.

The soldiers took him in charge, and he was marched away across the parade to the prison. This was a stone building, one story in height, with small grated windows, and stout oaken door studded with iron nails. Inside there were two rooms, one on each side of the entrance. These rooms were low, and the floor, which was laid on the earth, was composed of boards, which were decayed and moulded with damp. The ceiling was low, and the light but scanty. A stout table and stool formed the only furniture, while a bundle of mouldy straw in one corner was evidently intended to be his bed. Into this place Claude entered; the door was fastened, and he was left alone.

On finding himself alone in this place, he sat upon the stool, and for some time his thoughts were scarcely of a coherent kind. It was not easy for him to understand or realize his position, such a short interval had elapsed since he was enjoying the sweets of an interview with Mimi. The transition had been sudden and terrible. It had cast him down from the highest happiness to the lowest misery. A few moments ago, and all was bright hope; now all was black despair. Indeed, his present situation had an additional gloom from the very happiness which he had recently enjoyed, and in direct proportion to it. Had it not been for that last interview, he would not have known what he had lost.

Hope for himself there was none. Even under ordinary circumstances, there could hardly have been any chance of his escape; but now, after Cazeneau had so nearly lost his life, there could be nothing in store for him but sure and speedy death. He saw that he would most undoubtedly be tried, condemned, and executed here in Louisbourg, and that there was not the slightest hope that he would be sent to France for his trial.

Not long after Claude had been thrust into his prison, a party entered the citadel, bearing with them a litter, upon which reclined the form of a feeble and suffering man. It was Cazeneau. The wound which Claude had given him had not been fatal, after all; and he had recovered sufficiently to endure a long journey in this way; yet it had been a severe one, and had made great ravages in him. He appeared many years older. Formerly, he had not looked over forty; now he looked at least as old as Père Michel. His face was wan; his complexion a grayish pallor; his frame was emaciated and weak. As he was brought into the citadel, the commandant came out from his residence to meet him, accompanied by some servants, and by these the suffering man was borne into the house.

"All is ready, my dear count," said the commandant. "You will feel much better after you have some rest of the proper kind."

"But have you arrested him?" asked Cazeneau, earnestly.

"I have; he is safe now in prison."

"Very good. And now, Monsieur Le Commandant, if you will have the kindness to send me to my room —"

"Monsieur Le Commandant, you reign here now," said the other. "My authority is over since you have come, and you have only to give your orders."

"At any rate, *mon ami*, you must remain in power till I get some rest and sleep," said Cazeneau.

Rest, food, and, above all, a good night's sleep, had a very favorable effect upon Cazeneau, and on the following morning, when the commandant waited on him, he congratulated him on the improvement in his appearance. Cazeneau acknowledged that he felt better, and made very pointed inquiries about Mimi, which led to the recital of the circumstances of Claude's arrest in Mimi's presence. Whatever impression this may have made upon the hearer, he did not show it, but preserved an unchanged demeanor.

A conversation of a general nature now followed, turning chiefly upon affairs in France.

"You had a long voyage," remarked the commandant.

"Yes; and an unpleasant one. We left in March, but it seems longer than that; for it was in February that I left Versailles, only a little while after the death of his eminence."

"I fancy there will be a great change now in the policy of the government."

"O, of course. The peace policy is over. War with England must be. The king professes now to do like his predecessor, and govern without a minister; but we all know what that means. To do without a minister is one thing for Louis Quatorze, but another thing altogether for Louis Quinze. The Duchesse de Chateauroux will be minister — for the present. Then we have D'Aguesseau, D'Argenson, and Maurepas. O, there'll be war at once. I dare say it has already been declared. At any rate, it's best to act on that principle."

"Well, as to that, monsieur, we generally do act on that principle out here. But Fleury was a wonderful old man."

"Yes; but he died too soon."

"Too soon! What, at the age of ninety?"

"O, well, I meant too soon for me. Had he died ten years ago, or had he lived two years longer, I should not have come out here."

"I did not know that it was a matter of regret to monsieur."

"Regret?" said Cazeneau, in a querulous tone — "regret? Monsieur, one does not leave a place like Versailles for a place like Louisbourg without regrets."

"True," said the other, who saw that it was a sore subject.

"With Fleury I had influence; but with the present company at Versailles, it is — well, different; and I am better here. Out of sight, out of mind. It was one of Fleury's last acts — this appointment. I solicited it, for certain reasons; chiefly because I saw that he could not last long. Well, they'll have enough to think of without calling me to mind; for, if I'm not mistaken, the Queen of Hungary will find occupation enough for them."

After some further conversation of this kind, Cazeneau returned to the subject of Mimi, asking particularly about her life in Louisbourg, and whether Claude had seen her often. The information which he received on this point seemed to give him satisfaction.

"Does this young man claim to be a Montresor?" asked the commandant, "or is he merely interesting himself in the affairs of that family by way of an intrigue?"

"It is an intrigue," said Cazeneau. "He does not call himself Montresor openly, but I have reason to know that he is intending to pass himself off as the son and heir of the Count Eugene, who was outlawed nearly twenty years ago. Perhaps you have heard of that."

"O, yes; I remember all about that. His wife was a Huguenot, and both of them got off. His estates were confiscated. It was private enmity, I believe. Some one got a rich haul. Ha, ha, ha!"

At this Cazeneau's face turned as black as a thundercloud. The commandant saw that his remark had been an unfortunate one, and hastened to change the conversation.

"So this young fellow has a plan of that sort, you think. Of course he's put up by others — some wirepullers behind the scenes. Well, he's safe enough now, and he has that hanging over him which will put an end to this scheme, whoever may have started it."

At this Cazeneau recovered his former calmness, and smiled somewhat grimly.

"I can guess pretty well," said Cazeneau, "how this plot may have originated. You must know that when the Count de Montresor and his countess fled, they took with them a servant who had been their steward. This man's name was Motier. Now, both the count and countess died shortly after their arrival in America. The countess died first, somewhere in Canada, and then the count seemed to lose his reason; for he went off into the wilderness, and has never been heard of since. He must have perished at once. His steward, Motier, was then left. This man was a Huguenot and an incorrigible rascal. He found Canada too hot to hold him with his infidel Huguenot faith, and so he went among the English. I dare say that this Motier, ever since, has been concocting a plan by which he might make his fortune out of the Montresor estates. This Claude Motier is his son, and has, no doubt, been brought up by old Motier to believe that he is the son of the count; or else the young villain is his partner. You see his game now — don't you? He hired a schooner to take him here. He would have began his work here by getting some of you on his side, and gaining some influence, or money, perhaps, to begin with. Very well; what then? Why, then off he goes to France, where he probably intended to take advantage of the change in the ministry to push his claims, in the hope of making something out of them. And there is no doubt that, with his impudence, the young villain might have done something. And that reminds me to ask you whether you found anything at his lodgings."

" No, nothing."

" He should be searched. He must have some papers."

" He shall be searched to-night."

" I should have done that before. I left word to have that done before sending him from Grand Pré; but, as the fellow got off, why, of course that was no use. And I only hope he hasn't thought of destroying the papers. But if he has any, he won't want to destroy them till the last moment. Perhaps he won't even think of it."

"Do you suppose that this Motier has lived among the English all his life?"

"I believe so."

"Impossible!"

"Why so?"

"His manner, his accent, and his look are all as French as they can possibly be."

"How he has done it I am unable to conjecture. This Motier, père, must have been a man of superior culture, to have brought up such a very gentlemanly young fellow as this."

"Well, there is a difficulty about that. My opinion of the New Englanders is such that I do not think they would allow a man to live among them who looked so like a Frenchman."

"Bah! his looks are nothing; and they don't know what his French accent may be."

"Do you think, after all, that his own story is true about living in New England? May he not be some adventurer, who has drifted away from France of late years, and has come in contact with Motier? Or, better yet, may he not have been prepared for his part, and sent out by some parties in France, who are familiar with the whole Montresor business, and are playing a deep game?"

Cazeneau, at this, sat for a time in deep thought.

"Your suggestion," said he, at length, "is certainly a good one, and worth consideration. Yet I don't see how it can be so. No — for this reason: the captain of the schooner was certainly a New Englander, and he spoke in my hearing, on several occasions, as though this Motier was, like himself, a native of New England, and as one, too, whom he had known for years. Once he spoke as though he had known him from boyhood. I know enough English to understand that. Besides, this fellow's English is as perfect as his French. No, it cannot be possible that he has been sent out by any parties in France. He must have lived in New England nearly all his life, even if he was not born there; and I cannot agree with you."

"O, I only made the suggestion. It was merely a passing thought."

"Be assured this steward Motier has brought him up with an eye to using him for the very purpose on which he is now going."

"Do you suppose that Motier is alive?"

"Of course."

"He may be dead."

"And what then?"

"In that case this young fellow is not an agent of anybody, but is acting for himself."

"Even if that were so, I do not see what difference it would make. He has been educated for the part which he is now playing."

"Do you think," asked the commandant, after a pause, "that the Count de Montresor had a son?"

"Certainly not."

"He may have had, and this young fellow may be the one."

"That's what he says," said Cazeneau; "but he can never prove it; and, besides, it was impossible, for the count would never have left him as he did."

CHAPTER XX.

EXAMINATIONS.

CAZENEAU improved in health and strength every day. A week passed, during which period he devoted all his attention to himself, keeping quietly to his room, with the exception of an occasional walk in the sun, when the weather was warm, and letting Nature do all she could. The wound had been severe, though not mortal, and hardly what could be called even dangerous. The worst was already past on the journey to Louisbourg; and when once he had arrived there, he had but to wait for his strength to rally from the shock.

While thus waiting, he saw no one outside of the family of the commandant. Mimi was not interfered with. Claude received no communications from him for good or evil. Père Michel, who expected to be put through a course of questioning, remained unquestioned; nor did he assume the office of commandant, which now was his.

At the end of a week he found himself so much better that he began to think himself able to carry out the various purposes which lay in his mind. First of all, he relieved the late commandant of his office, and took that dignity upon himself.

All this time Mimi had been under the same roof,

a prey to the deepest anxiety. The poignant grief which she had felt for the loss of her father had been alleviated for a time by the escape of Claude; but now, since his arrest, and the arrival of the dreaded Cazeneau, it seemed worse than ever; the old grief returned, and, in addition, there were new ones of equal force. There was the terror about her own future, which looked dark indeed before her, from the purposes of Cazeneau; and then there was also the deep anxiety, which never left her, about the fate of Claude. Of him she knew nothing, having heard not one word since his arrest. She had not seen Père Michel, and there was no one whom she could ask. The lady of the commandant was kind enough; but to Mimi she seemed a mere creature of Cazeneau, and for this reason she never dreamed of taking her into her confidence, though that good lady made several unmistakable attempts to enter into her secret.

Such was her state of mind when she received a message that M. Le Comte de Cazeneau wished to pay his respects to her.

Mimi knew only too well what that meant, and would have avoided the interview under any plea whatever, if it had been possible. But that could not be done; and so, with a heart that throbbed with painful emotions, she went to meet him.

After waiting a little time, Cazeneau made his appearance, and greeted her with very much warmth and earnestness. He endeavored to infuse into his manner as much as possible of the cordiality of an old and tried friend, together with the tenderness which might be shown by a father or an elder brother. He was careful not to exhibit the slightest trace of annoyance at anything that had happened since he last saw her, nor to show any suspicion that she could be in any way implicated with his enemy.

But Mimi did not meet him half way. She was cold and repellent; or, rather, perhaps it may with more truth be said, she was frightened and embarrassed.

In spite of Cazeneau's determination to touch on nothing unpleasant, he could not help noticing Mimi's reserve, and remarking on it.

"You do not congratulate me," said he. "Perhaps you have not heard the reason why I left your party in the woods. It was not because I grew tired of your company. It was because I was attacked by an assassin, and narrowly escaped with my life. It has only been by a miracle that I have come here; and, though I still have something of my strength, yet I am very far from being the man that I was when you saw me last."

At these words Mimi took another look at Cazeneau, and surveyed him somewhat more closely. She felt a slight shock at noticing now the change which had taken place in him. He looked so haggard, and so old!

She murmured a few words, which Cazeneau accepted as expressions of good will, and thanked her accordingly. The conversation did not last much longer. Cazeneau himself found it rather too tedious where he had to do all the talking, and where the other was only a girl too sad or too sullen to answer. One final remark was made, which seemed to Mimi to express the whole purpose of his visit.

"You need not fear, mademoiselle," said he, "that

this assassin will escape. That is impossible, since he is under strict confinement, and in a few days must be tried for his crimes."

What that meant Mimi knew only too well; and after Cazeneau left, these words rang in her heart.

After his call on Mimi, Cazeneau was waited on by the ex-commandant, who acquainted him with the result of certain inquiries which he had been making. These inquiries had been made by means of a prisoner, who had been put in with Claude in order to win the young man's confidence, and thus get at his secret; for Cazeneau had been of the opinion that there were accomplices or allies of Claude in France, of whom it would be well to know the names. The ex-commandant was still more eager to know. He had been very much struck by the claim of Claude to be a De Montresor, and by Cazeneau's own confession that the present *régime* was unfavorable to him; and under these circumstances the worthy functionary, who always looked out for number one, was busy weighing the advantages of the party of Claude as against the party of Cazeneau.

On the evening of the day when he had called on Mimi, Cazeneau was waited on by Père Michel. He himself had sent for the priest, whom he had summoned somewhat abruptly. The priest entered the apartment, and, with a bow, announced himself. As Cazeneau looked up, he appeared for a moment struck with involuntary respect by the venerable appearance of this man, or there may have been something else at work in him; but, whatever the cause, he regarded the priest attentively for a few moments, without saying a word.

"Père Michel," said he, at length, "I have called you before me in private, to come to an understanding with you. Had I followed my own impulses, I would have ordered your arrest, on my entrance into Louisbourg, as an accomplice of that young villain. I thought it sufficient, however, to spare you for the present, and keep you under surveillance. I am, on the whole, glad that I did not yield to my first impulse of anger, for I can now, in perfect calmness, go with you over your acts during the journey here, and ask you for an explanation."

The priest bowed.

"Understand me, Père Michel," said Cazeneau; "I have now no hard feeling left. I may say, I have almost no suspicion. I wish to be assured of your innocence. I will take anything that seems like a plausible excuse. I respect your character, and would rather have you as my friend than — than not."

The priest again bowed, without appearing at all affected by these conciliatory words.

"After I was assassinated in the woods," said Cazeneau, "I was saved from death by the skill and fidelity of my Indians. It seems to me still, Père Michel, as it seemed then, that something might have been done by you. Had you been in league with my enemy, you could not have done worse. You hastened forward with all speed, leaving me to my fate. As a friend, you should have turned back to save a friend; as a priest, you should have turned back to give me Christian burial. What answer have you to make to this?"

"Simply this," said the priest, with perfect calmness: "that when you left us you gave orders that we should go on, and that you would find your way to us.

I had no thought of turning back, or waiting. I knew the Indians well, and knew that they can find their way through the woods as easily as you can through the streets of Paris. I went forward, then, without any thought of waiting for you, thinking that of course you would join us, as you said."

"When did Motier come up with you?" asked Cazeneau.

"On the following day," answered the priest.

"Did he inform you what had taken place?"

"He did."

"Why, then, did you not turn back to help me?"

"Because Motier informed me that you were dead."

"Very good. He believed so, I doubt not; but, at any rate, you might have turned back, if only to give Christian burial."

"I intended to do that at some future time," said Père Michel; "but at that time I felt my chief duty to be to the living. How could I have left the Countess Laborde? Motier would not have been a proper guardian to convey her to Louisbourg, and to take her back with me was impossible. I therefore decided to go on, as you said, and take her first to Louisbourg, and afterwards to return."

"You showed no haste about it," said Cazeneau.

"I had to wait here," said the priest.

"May I ask what could have been the urgent business which kept you from the sacred duty of the burial of the dead?"

"A ship is expected every day, and I waited to get the letters of my superiors, with reference to further movements on my mission."

"You say that Motier informed you about my death. Did he tell you how it had happened?"

"He said that you and he had fought, and that you had been killed."

"Why, then, did you not denounce him to the authorities on your arrival here?"

"On what charge?"

"On the charge of murder."

"I did not know that when one gentleman is unfortunate enough to kill another, in fair fight, that it can be considered murder. The duel is as lawful in America as in France."

"This was not a duel!" cried Cazeneau. "It was an act of assassination. Motier is no better than a murderer."

"I only knew his own account," said the priest.

"Besides," continued Cazeneau, "a duel can only take place between two equals; and this Motier is one of the *canaille*, one not worthy of my sword."

"Yet, monsieur," said the priest, "when you arrested him first, it was not as one of the *canaille*, but as the son of the outlawed Count de Montresor."

"True," said Cazeneau; "but I have reason to believe that he is merely some impostor. He is now under a different accusation. But one more point. How did Motier manage to escape?"

"As to that, monsieur, I always supposed that his escape was easy enough, and that he could have effected it at once. The farm-houses of the Acadians are not adapted to be very secure prisons. There were no bolts and bars, and no adequate watch."

"True; but the most significant part of his escape is, that he had external assistance. Who were those Indians who led him on my trail? How did he, a stranger, win them over?"

"You forget, monsieur, that this young man has lived all his life in America. I know that he has been much in the woods in New England, and has had much intercourse with the Indians there. It was, no doubt, very easy for him to enter into communication with Indians here. They are all alike."

"But how could he have found them? He must have had them at the house, or else friends outside must have sent them."

"He might have bribed the people of the house."

"Impossible!"

"Monsieur does not mean to say that anything is impossible to one who has gold. Men of this age do anything for gold."

Cazeneau was silent. To him this was so profoundly true that he had nothing to say. He sat in silence for a little while, and then continued: —

"I understand that at the time of the arrest of Motier, he was in the garden of the residence, with the Countess de Laborde, and that you were with them. How is this? Did this interview take place with your sanction or connivance?"

"I knew nothing about it. It was by the merest accident, as far as I know."

"You did not help them in this way?"

"I did not."

"Monsieur L'Abbé," said Cazeneau, "I am glad that you have answered my questions so fully and so frankly. I confess that, in my first anger, I considered that in some way you had taken part against me. To think so gave me great pain, as I have had too high an esteem for you to be willing to think of you as an enemy. But your explanations are in every way satisfactory. I hope, monsieur, that whatever letters you receive from France, they will not take you away from this part of the world. I feel confident that you, with your influence over the Indians here, will be an invaluable ally to one in my position, in the endeavors which I shall make to further in these parts the interests of France and of the church."

CHAPTER XXI.

A RAY OF LIGHT.

AFTER leaving Cazeneau, Père Michel went to the prison where Claude was confined. The young man looked pale and dejected, for the confinement had told upon his health and spirits; and worse than the confinement was the utter despair which had settled down upon his soul. At the sight of the priest, he gave a cry of joy, and hurried forward.

"I thought you had forgotten all about me," said Claude, as he embraced the good priest, while tears of joy started to his eyes.

"I have never forgotten you, my son," said the priest, as he returned his embrace; "that is impossible. I have thought of you both night and day, and have been trying to do something for you."

"For me," said Claude, gloomily, "nothing can be done. But tell me about her. How does she bear this?"

"Badly," said the priest, "as you may suppose."

Claude sighed.

"My son," said the priest, "I have come to you now on important business; and, first of all, I wish to speak to you about a subject that you will consider most important. I mean that secret which you wish to discover, and which drew you away from your home."

"Do you know anything about it?"

"Much. Remember I was with Laborde in his last hours, and received his confession. I am, therefore, able to tell you all that you wish to know; and after that you must decide for yourself another question, which will grow out of this.

"About twenty years ago there was a beautiful heiress, who was presented at court. Her name was the Countess de Besançon. She was a Huguenot, and therefore not one whom you would expect to see amid the vicious circles at Versailles. But her guardians were Catholic, and hoped that the attractions of the court might weaken her faith. She became the admired of all, and great was the rivalry for her favor. Two, in particular, devoted themselves to her — the Count de Montresor and the Count de Laborde. She preferred the former, and they were married. After this, the count and countess left the court, and retired to the Chateau de Montresor.

"Laborde and Montresor had always been firm friends until this; but now Laborde, stung by jealousy and hate, sought to effect the ruin of Montresor. At first his feeling was only one of jealousy, which was not unnatural, under the circumstances. Left to himself, I doubt not that it would have died a natural death; but, unfortunately, Laborde was under the influence of a crafty adventurer, who now, when Montresor's friendship was removed, gained an ascendency over him. This man was this Cazeneau, who has treated you so shamefully.

"I will not enlarge upon his character. You yourself know now well enough what that is. He was a man of low origin, who had grown up amid the vilest court on the surface of the earth. At that time the Duke of Orleans and the Abbé Dubois had control of everything, and the whole court was an infamous scene of corruption. Cazeneau soon found means to turn the jealousy of Laborde into a deeper hate, and to gain his co-operation in a scheme which he had formed for his own profit.

"Cazeneau's plan was this: The laws against the Huguenots were very stringent, and were in force, as, indeed, they are yet. The Countess de Montresor was a Huguenot, and nothing could make her swerve from her faith. The first blow was levelled at her, for in this way they knew that they could inflict a deeper wound upon her husband. She was to be arrested, subjected to the mockery of French justice, and condemned to the terrible punishment which the laws inflicted upon heretics. Had Montresor remained at court, he could easily have fought off this pair of conspirators; but, being away, he knew nothing about it till all was ready; and then he had nothing to do but to fly, in order to save his wife.

"Upon this, fresh charges were made against him, and lettres de cachet were issued. These would have flung him into the Bastile, to rot and die forgotten. But Montresor had effectually concealed himself, together with his wife, and the emissaries of the government were baffled. It was by that time too late for him to defend himself in any way; and the end of it was, that he decided to fly from France. He did so, and succeeded in reaching Quebec in safety. Here he hoped to remain only for a time, and expected that before long a change in the ministry might take place, by means of which he might regain his rights.

"But Fleury was all-powerful with the king, and Cazeneau managed somehow to get into Fleury's good graces, so that Montresor had no chance. The Montresor estates, and all the possessions of his wife, were confiscated, and Laborde and Cazeneau secured much of them. But Montresor had other things to trouble him. His wife grew ill, and died not long after his arrival, leaving an infant son. Montresor now had nothing which seemed to him worth living for. He therefore left his child to the care of the faithful Mother, and disappeared, as you have told me, and has never been heard of since.

"Of course Laborde knew nothing of this, and I only add this to the information which he gave, in order to make it as plain to you as it is to me. Laborde asserted that after the first blow he recoiled, conscience-stricken, and refused further to pursue your father, though Cazeneau was intent upon his complete destruction; and perhaps this is the reason why Montresor was not molested at Quebec. A better reason, however, is to be found in the merciful nature of Fleury, whom I believe at bottom to have been a good man.

"After this, years passed. To Laborde they were years of remorse. Hoping to get rid of his misery, he married. A daughter was born to him. It was of no use. His wife died. His daughter was sent to a convent to be educated. He himself was a lonely, aimless man. What was worse, he was always under the power of Cazeneau, who never would let go his hold. This Cazeneau squandered the plunder of the Montresors upon his own vices, and soon became as poor as he was originally. After this he lived upon Laborde.

His knowledge of Laborde's remorse gave him a power over him which his unhappy victim could not resist. The false information which Laborde had sworn to against the Count de Montresor was perjury; and Cazeneau, the very man who had suggested it, was always ready to threaten to denounce him to Fleury.

"So time went on. Laborde grew older, and at last the one desire of his life was to make amends before he died. At length Fleury died. The new ministry were different. All of them detested Cazeneau. One of them — Maurepas — was a friend to Laborde. To this Maurepas, Laborde told his whole story, and Maurepas promised that he would do all in his power to make amends. The greatest desire of Laborde was to discover some one of the family. He had heard that the count and countess were both dead, but that they had left an infant son. It was this that brought him out here. He hoped to find that son, and perhaps the count himself, for the proof of his death was not very clear. He did, indeed, find that son, most wonderfully, too, and without knowing it; for, as you yourself see, there cannot be a doubt that you are that son.

"Now, Laborde kept all this a profound secret from Cazeneau, and hoped, on leaving France, never to see him again. What, however, was his amazement, on reaching the ship, to learn that Cazeneau also was going! He had got the appointment to Louisbourg from Fleury before his death, and the appointment had been confirmed by the new ministry, for some reason or other. I believe that they will recall him at once, and use his absence to effect his ruin. I believe Cazeneau expects this, and is trying to strengthen his resources by getting control of the Laborde estates.

His object in marrying Mimi is simply this. This was the chief dread of Laborde in dying, and with his last words he entreated me to watch over his daughter.

"Cazeneau's enmity to you must be accounted for on the ground that he discovered, somehow, your parentage. Mimi told me afterwards, that he was near you one day, concealed, while you were telling her. He was listening, beyond a doubt, and on the first opportunity determined to put you out of the way. He dreads, above all things, your appearance in France as the son of the unfortunate Count de Montresor. For now all those who were once powerful are dead, and the present government would be very glad to espouse the Montresor cause, and make amends, as far as possible, for his wrongs. They would like to use you as a means of dealing a destructive blow against Cazeneau himself. Cazeneau's first plan was to put you out of the way on some charge of treason; but now, of course, the charge against you will be attempt at murder."

To all this Claude listened with much less interest than he would have felt formerly. But the sentence of death seemed impending, and it is not surprising that the things of this life seemed of small moment.

"Well," said he, with a sigh, "I'm much obliged to you for telling me all this; but it makes very little difference to me now."

"Wait till you have heard all," said the priest. "I have come here for something more; but it was necessary to tell you all this at the first. I have now to tell you that — your position is full of hope; in fact — " Here the priest put his head close to Claude's ear, and whispered, "I have come to save you."

"What!" cried Claude.

The priest placed his hand on Claude's mouth.

"No one is listening; but it is best to be on our guard," he whispered. "Yes, I can save you, and will. This very night you shall be free, on your way to join your friend, the captain. To-day I received a message from him by an Indian. He had reached Canso. I had warned him to go there. The Indians went on board, and brought his message. He will wait there for us."

At this intelligence, which to Claude was unexpected and amazing, he could not say one word, but sat with clasped hands and a face of rapture. But suddenly a thought came to his mind, which disturbed his joy.

"Mimi — what of her?"

"You must go alone," said the priest.

Claude's face grew dark. He shook his head.

"Then I will not go at all."

"Not go! Who is she — do you know? She is the daughter of Laborde, the man who ruined your father."

Claude compressed his lips, and looked with fixed determination at the priest.

"She is not to blame," said he, "for her father's faults. She has never known them, and never shall know them. Besides, for all that he did, her father suffered, and died while seeking to make atonement. My father himself, were he alive, would surely forgive that man for all he did; and I surely will not cherish hate against his memory. So Mimi shall be mine. She is mine; we have exchanged vows. I will stay here and die, rather than go and leave her."

"Spoken like a young fool, as you are!" said the priest. "Well, if you will not go without her, you shall go with her; but go you must, and to-night."

"What? can she go too, after all? O, my best Père Michel, what can I say?"

"Say nothing as yet, for there is one condition."

"What is that? I will agree to anything. Never mind conditions."

"You must be married before you go."

"Married!" cried Claude, in amazement.

"Yes."

"Married! How? Am I not here in a dungeon? How can she and I be married?"

"I will tell you how presently. But first, let me tell you why. First of all, we may all get scattered in the woods. It will be very desirable that she should have you for her lawful lord and master, so that you can have a right to stand by her to the last. You can do far more for her than I can, and I do not wish to have all the responsibility. This is one reason.

"But there is another reason, which, to me, is of greater importance. It is this, my son: You may be captured. The worst may come to the worst. You may — which may Heaven forbid — yet you may be put to death. I do not think so. I hope not. I hope, indeed, that Cazeneau may eventually fall a prey to his own machinations. But it is necessary to take this into account. And then, my son, if such a sad fate should indeed be yours, we must both of us think what will be the fate of Mimi. If you are not married, her fate will be swift and certain. She will be forced to marry this infamous miscreant, who does not even pretend to love her, but merely wants her money. He has already told her his intention — telling her that her father left nothing, and that he wishes to save her from want, whereas her father left a very large estate. Such will be her fate if she is single. But if she is your wife, all will be different. As your widow, she will be safe. He would have to allow her a decent time for mourning; and in any case he would scarce be able so to defy public opinion as to seek to marry the widow of the man whom he had killed. Besides, to gain time would be everything; and before a year would be over, a host of friends would spring up to save her from him. This, then, is the reason why I think that you should be married."

"I am all amazement," cried Claude, "I am bewildered. Married! Such a thing would be my highest wish. But I don't understand all this. How is it possible to think of marriage at such a time as this?"

"Well, I will now explain that," said the priest. "The late commandant is a friend of mine. We were acquainted with each other years ago in France. As soon as Cazeneau made his appearance here, and you were arrested, I went to him and told him the whole story of your parents, as I have just now told you. He had heard something about their sad fate in former years, and his sympathies were all enlisted. Besides, he looks upon Cazeneau as a doomed man, the creature of the late *régime*, the fallen government. He expects that Cazeneau will be speedily recalled, disgraced, and punished. He also expects that the honors of the Count de Montresor will be restored to you. He is sufficient of an aristocrat to prefer an old and honorable name, like Montresor, to that of a low and unprincipled adventurer, like Cazeneau, and does not wish to see the Countess Laborde fall a victim to the machinations of a worn-out scoundrel. And so the ex-commandant will do all that he can. Were it not for him, I do not think I could succeed in freeing both of you, though I still might contrive to free you alone."

"O, my dear Père Michel! What can I say? I am dumb!"

"Say nothing. I must go now."

"When will you come?"

"At midnight. There will be a change of guards then. The new sentry will be favorable; he will run away with us, so as to save himself from punishment."

"And when shall we be married?"

"To-night. You will go from here to the commandant's residence, and then out. But we must haste, for by daybreak Cazeneau will discover all — perhaps before. We can be sure, however, of three hours. I hope it will be light. Well, we must trust to Providence. And now, my son, farewell till midnight."

CHAPTER XXII.

ESCAPE.

CLAUDE remained alone once more, with his brain in a whirl from the tumult of thought which had arisen. This interview with the priest had been the most eventful hour of his life. He had learned the secret of his parentage, the wrongs and sufferings of his father and mother, the villany of Cazeneau, the true reason for the bitter enmity which in him had triumphed over gratitude, and made him seek so pertinaciously the life of the man who had once saved his own.

It seemed like a dream. But a short time before, not one ray of hope appeared to illuminate the midnight gloom which reigned around him and within him. Now all was dazzling brightness. It seemed too bright; it was unnatural; it was too much to hope for. That he should escape was of itself happiness enough; but that he should also join Mimi once more, and that he should be joined to her, no more to part till death, was an incredible thing. Mimi herself must also know this, and was even now waiting for him, as he was waiting for her.

Claude waited in a fever of impatience. The monotonous step of the sentry sounded out as he paced to and fro. At times Claude thought he heard the approach of footsteps, and listened eagerly; but over and over again he was compelled to desist, on finding that his senses deceived him. Thus the time passed, and as it passed, his impatience grew the more uncontrollable. Had it been possible, he would have burst open the door, and ventured forth so as to shorten his suspense.

At length a sound of approaching footsteps did in reality arise. This time there was no mistake. He heard voices outside, the challenge and reply of the changing guard. Then footsteps departed, and the tramp died away, leaving only the pacing of the sentinel for Claude to hear. What now? Was this the sentinel who was to be his friend? He thought so. He believed so. The time passed — too long a time, he thought, for the sentinel gave no sign: still he kept up his monotonous tramp. Claude repressed his impatience, and waited till, to his astonishment, what seemed an immense time, had passed away; and the sentinel came not to his aid.

Still the time passed. Claude did not know what to think. Gradually a sickening fear arose — the fear that the whole plan had been discovered, and that the priest had failed. Perhaps the commandant had played him false, and had pretended to sympathize with him so as to draw out his purpose, which he would reveal to Cazeneau, in order to gain his gratitude, and lay him under obligation. The priest, he thought, was too guileless to deal with men of the world like these. He had been caught in a trap, and had involved himself with all the rest. His own fate could be no worse than it was before, but it was doubly bitter to fall back into his despair, after having been for a brief interval raised up to so bright a hope.

Such were the thoughts that finally took possession of Claude, and, with every passing moment, deepened into conviction. Midnight had passed; the sentry had come, and there he paced mechanically, with no thought of him. Either the ex-commandant or the sentinel had betrayed them. Too many had been in the secret. Better never to have heard of this plan than, having heard of it, to find it thus dashed away on the very eve of its accomplishment. Time passed, and every moment only added to Claude's bitterness; time passed, and every moment only served to show him that all was over. A vague thought came of speaking to the sentinel; but that was dismissed. Then another thought came, of trying to tear away the iron grating; but the impossibility of that soon showed itself. He sank down upon his litter of straw in one corner, and bade adieu to hope. Then he started up, and paced up and down wildly, unable to yield so calmly to despair. Then once more he sank down upon the straw.

Thus he was lying, crouched down, his head in his hands, overwhelmed utterly, when suddenly a deep sound came to his ears, which in an instant made him start to his feet, and drove away every despairing thought, bringing in place of these a new wave of hope, and joy, and amazement. It was the single toll of the great bell, which, as he knew, always sounded at midnight.

Midnight! Was it possible? Midnight had not passed, then. The change of sentry had been at nine o'clock, which he, deceived by the slow progress of the hours, had supposed to be midnight. He had been mistaken. There was yet hope. He rushed to the grating, and listened. There were footsteps approaching — the tramp of the relieving guard. He listened till the guard was relieved, and the departing footsteps died away. Then began the pace of the new sentry.

What now? Was there to be a repetition of his former experience? Was he again to be dashed down from this fresh hope into a fresh despair? He nerved himself for this new ordeal, and waited with a painfully throbbing heart. At the grating he stood, motionless, listening, with all his soul wrapped and absorbed in his single sense of hearing. There were an inner grating and an outer one, and between the two a sash with two panes of glass. He could hear the sentry as he paced up and down; he could also hear, far away, the long, shrill note of innumerable frogs; and the one seemed as monotonous, as unchangeable, and as interminable as the other.

But at length the pacing of the sentry ceased. Claude listened; the sentinel stopped; there was no longer any sound. Claude listened still. This was the supreme hour of his fate. On this moment depended all his future. What did this mean? Would the sentry begin his tramp?

He would; he did. In despair Claude fled from the grating, and fell back upon the straw. For a time he seemed unconscious of everything; but at length he was roused by a rattle at the door of his cell. In a moment he was on his feet, listening. It was the sound of a key as it slowly turned in the lock. Claude moved not, spoke not; he waited. If this was his deliverer, all well; if not, he was resolved to have a struggle for freedom. Then he stole cautiously to the door.

It opened. Claude thrust his hand through, and seized a human arm. A man's voice whispered back, —

"*H-s-s-t! Suivez moi.*"

A thrill of rapture unutterable passed through every nerve and fibre of Claude. At once all the past was forgotten; forgotten, also, were all the dangers that still lay before him. It was enough that this hope had not been frustrated, that the sentinel had come to deliver him from the cell at the midnight hour. The cool breeze of night was wafted in through the open door, and fanned the fevered brow of the prisoner, bearing on its wings a soothing influence, a healing balm, and life, and hope. His presence of mind all came back: he was self-poised, vigilant, cool: all this in one instant. All his powers would be needed to carry him through the remainder of the night; and these all were summoned forth, and came at his bidding. And so Claude followed his guide.

The sentinel led the way, under the shadow of the wall, towards the Residency. At one end of this was the chapel. Towards this the sentinel guided Claude, and, on reaching it, opened the door. A hand seized his arm, a voice whispered in his ear, —

"Welcome, my son. Here is your bride."

And then a soft hand was placed in his. Claude knew whose hand it was. He flung his arms around the slender figure of Mimi, and pressed her to his heart.

"Come," said the priest.

He drew them up towards the altar. Others were present. Claude could not see them; one, however, he could see, was a female, whom he supposed to be

Margot. The moonlight shone in through the great window over the altar. Here the priest stood, and placed Claude and Mimi before him.

Then he went through the marriage service. It was a strange wedding there at midnight, in the moonlit chapel, with the forms of the spectators so faintly discerned, and the ghostly outline of priest, altar, and window before them as they knelt. But they were married; and Claude once more, in a rapture of feeling, pressed his wife to his heart.

They now left the chapel by another door in the rear. The priest led the way, together with the sentinel. Here was the wall. A flight of steps led to the top. On reaching this they came to a place where there was a ladder. Down this they all descended in silence, and found themselves in the ditch. The ladder was once more made use of to climb out of this, and then Claude saw a figure crouched on the ground and creeping towards them. It was an Indian, with whom the priest conversed in his own language for a moment.

"All is well," he whispered to Claude. "The captain is waiting for us many miles from this. And now, forward!"

The Indian led the way; then went the priest; then Claude with Mimi; then Margot; last of all came the sentinel, who had deserted his post, and was now seeking safety in flight under the protection of Père Michel. Such was the little party of fugitives that now sought to escape from Louisbourg into the wild forest around. After walking for about a mile, they reached a place where five horses were bound. Here they proceeded to mount.

"I sent these out after sundown," said the priest to Claude. "There are not many horses in Louisbourg. These will assist us to escape, and will be lost to those who pursue. Here, my son, arm yourself, so as to defend your wife, in case of need."

With these words the priest handed Claude a sword, pointing also to pistols which were in the holster. The Indian alone remained on foot. He held the bridle of the priest's horse, and led the way, sometimes on what is called an "Indian trot," at other times on a walk. The others all followed at the same pace.

The road was the same one which had been traversed by Claude and Mimi when they first came to Louisbourg — a wide trail, rough, yet serviceable, over which many pack-horses and droves of cattle had passed, but one which was not fitted for wheels, and was rather a trail than a road. On each side the trees arose, which threw a deep shade, so that, in spite of the moon which shone overhead, it was too dark to go at any very rapid pace.

"We must make all the haste we can," said the priest. "In three hours they will probaby discover all. The alarm will be given, and we shall be pursued. In these three hours, then, we must get so far ahead that they may not be able to come up with us."

At first the pathway was wide enough for them all to move at a rapid pace; but soon it began to grow narrower. As they advanced, the trees grew taller, and the shadows which they threw were darker. The path became more winding, for, like all trails, it avoided the larger trees or stones, and wound around them, where a road would have led to their removal.

The path also became rougher, from stones which protruded in many places, or from long roots stretching across, which in the darkness made the horses stumble incessantly. These it was impossible to avoid. In addition to these, there were miry places, where the horses sank deep, and could only extricate themselves with difficulty.

Thus their progress grew less and less, till at length it dwindled to a walk, and a slow one at that. Nothing else could be done. They all saw the impossibility of more rapid progress, in the darkness, over such a path. Of them all, Claude was the most impatient, as was natural. His sense of danger was most keen. The terror of the night had not yet passed away. Already, more than once, he had gone from despair to hope, and back once more to despair; and it seemed to him as though his soul must still vibrate between these two extremes. The hope which was born out of new-found freedom was now rapidly yielding to the fear of pursuit and re-capture.

In the midst of these thoughts, he came forth suddenly upon a broad, open plain, filled with stout underbrush. Through this the trail ran. Reaching this, the whole party urged their horses at full speed, and for at least three miles they were able to maintain this rapid progress. At the end of that distance, the trail once more entered the woods, and the pace dwindled to a walk. But that three-mile run cheered the spirits of all.

"How many miles have we come, I wonder?" asked Claude.

"About six," said the priest.

"How many miles is it to the schooner?"

"About forty."

Claude drew a long breath.

"It must be nearly three o'clock in the morning now," said he. "I dare say they are finding it out now."

"Well, we needn't stop to listen," said the priest.

"No; we'll hear them soon enough."

"At any rate, the dawn is coming," said the priest. "The day will soon be here, and then we can go on as fast as we wish."

CHAPTER XXIII.

PURSUIT.

AS they hurried on, it grew gradually lighter, so that they were able to advance more rapidly. The path remained about the same, winding as before, and with the same alternations of roots, stones, and swamp; but the daylight made all the difference in the world, and they were now able to urge their horses at the top of their speed. The Indian who was at their head was able to keep there without much apparent effort, never holding back or falling behind, though if the ground had been smoother he could scarcely have done so. With every step the dawn advanced, until at last the sun rose, and all the forest grew bright in the beams of day. A feeling of hope and joy succeeded to the late despondency which had been creeping over them; but this only stimulated them to redoubled exertions, so that they might not, after all, find themselves at last cheated out of these bright hopes.

That they were now pursued they all felt confident. At three o'clock the absence of the sentry must have been discovered, and, of course, the flight of Claude. Thereupon the alarm would at once be given. Cazeneau would probably be aroused, and would proceed to take action immediately. Even under what might be the most favorable circumstances to them, it was not likely that there would be a delay of more than an hour.

Besides, the pursuer had an advantage over them. They had a start of three hours; but those three hours were spent in darkness, when they were able to go over but little ground. All that they had toiled so long in order to traverse, their pursuers could pass over in one quarter the time, and one quarter the labor. They were virtually not more than one hour in advance of the enemy, who would have fresher horses, with which to lessen even this small advantage. And by the most favorable calculation, there remained yet before them at least thirty miles, over a rough and toilsome country. Could they hope to escape?

Such were the thoughts that came to Claude's mind, and such the question that came to him. That question he did not care to discuss with himself. He could only resolve to keep up the flight till the last moment, and then resist to the bitter end.

But now there arose a new danger, which brought fresh difficulties with it, and filled Claude with new despondency. This danger arose from a quarter in which he was most assailable to fear and anxiety — from Mimi.

He had never ceased, since they first left, to watch over his bride with the most anxious solicitude, sometimes riding by her side and holding her hand, when the path admitted it, at other times riding behind her, so as to keep her in view, and all the time never ceasing to address to her words of comfort and good cheer. To all his questions Mimi had never failed to respond in a voice which was full of cheerfulness and sprightliness, and no misgivings on her account entered his mind until the light grew bright enough for him to see her face. Then he was struck by her appearance. She seemed so feeble, so worn, so fatigued, that a great fear came over him.

"O, Mimi, darling!" he cried, "this is too much for you."

"O, no," she replied, in the same tone; "I can keep up as long as you wish me to."

"But you look so completely worn out!"

"O, that's because I've been fretting about you — you bad boy; it's not this ride at all."

"Are you sure that you can keep up?"

"Why, of course I am; and I must, for there's nothing else to be done."

"O, Mimi, I'm afraid — I'm very much afraid that you will break down."

At this Mimi gave a little laugh, but said nothing, and Claude found himself compelled to trust to hope. Thus they went on for some time longer.

But at length Claude was no longer able to conceal the truth from himself, nor was Mimi able any longer to maintain her loving deception. She was exceedingly weak; she was utterly worn out; and in pain Claude saw her form sway to and fro and tremble. He asked her imploringly to stop and rest. But at the sound of his voice, Mimi roused herself once more, by a great effort.

"O, no," she said, with a strong attempt to speak unconcernedly; "O, no. I acknowledge I am a little tired; and if we come to any place where we may rest, I think I shall do so; but not here, not here; let us go farther."

Claude drew a long breath. Deep anxiety overwhelmed him. Mimi was, in truth, right. How could they dare to pause just here? The pursuer was on their track! No; they must keep on; and if Mimi did sink, what then? But he would not think of it; he would hope that Mimi would be able, after all, to hold out.

But at length what Claude had feared came to pass. He had been riding behind Mimi for some time, so as to watch her better, when suddenly he saw her slender frame reel to one side. A low cry came from her. In an instant Claude was at her side, and caught her in his arms in time to save her from a fall.

Mimi had not fainted, but was simply prostrated from sheer fatigue. No strength was left, and it was impossible for her to sit up any longer. She had struggled to bear up as long as possible, and finally had given way altogether.

"I cannot help it," she murmured.

"O, my darling!" cried Claude, in a voice of anguish.

"Forgive me, dear Claude. I cannot help it!"

"O, don't talk so," said Claude. "I ought to have seen your weakness before, and given you assistance. But come now; I will hold you in my arms, and we will still be able to go on."

"I wish you would leave me; only leave me, and then you can be saved. There is no danger for me; but if you are captured, your life will be taken. O, Claude, dearest Claude, leave me and fly."

"You distress me, Mimi, darling, by all this. I cannot leave you; I would rather die than do so. And so, if you love me, don't talk so."

At this, with a little sob, Mimi relapsed into silence.

"Courage, darling," said Claude, in soothing tones. "Who knows but that they are still in Louisbourg, and have not yet left? We may get away, after all; or we may find some place of hiding."

The additional burden which he had been forced to assume overweighted very seriously Claude's horse, and signs of this began to appear before long. No sooner, however, had Claude perceived that it was difficult to keep with the rest of the party, than he concluded to shift himself, with Mimi, to the horse which Mimi had left. This was one of the best and freshest of the whole party, and but a slight delay was occasioned by the change.

After this they kept up a good rate of speed for more than two hours, when Claude once more changed to another horse. This time it was to Margot's horse, which had done less thus far than any of the others. Margot then took the horse which Claude had at first, and thus they went on. It was a good contrivance, for thus by changing about from one to another, and by allowing one horse to be led, the endurance of the whole was maintained longer than would otherwise have been possible.

But at length the long and fatiguing journey began to tell most seriously on all the horses, and all began to see that further progress would not be much longer possible. For many hours they had kept on their path; and, though the distance which they had gone was not more than twenty-five miles, yet, so rough had been the road that the labor had been excessive, and all the horses needed rest. By this time it was midday, and they all found themselves face to face with a question of fearful import, which none of them knew how to answer. The question was, what to do. Could they stop? Dare they? Yet they must. For the present they continued on a little longer.

They now came to another open space, overgrown with shrubbery, similar to that which they had traversed in the night. It was about two miles in extent, and at the other end arose a bare, rocky hill, beyond which was the forest.

"We must halt at the top of that hill," said Claude. "It's the best place. We can guard against a surprise, at any rate. Some of the horses will drop if we go on much farther."

"I suppose we'll have to," said the priest.

"We must rest for half an hour, at least," said Claude. "If they come up, we'll have to scatter, and take to the woods."

With these words they rode on, and at length reached the hill. The path wound up it, and in due time they reached the top.

But scarcely had they done so, than a loud cry sounded out, which thrilled through all hearts. Immediately after, a figure came bounding towards them.

"Hooray! Hip, hip, hooray!" shouted the new comer.

"Heavens! Zac!" cried Claude; "you here?"

"Nobody else," replied Zac, wringing his hand. "But what are you going to do?"

"Our horses are blown; we are pursued, but have to halt for a half hour or so. If they come up, we'll have to scatter, and take to the woods, and start the horses ahead on the path. This is a good lookout place."

With these words Claude began to dismount, bearing his beloved burden. The priest assisted him. Zac, after his first hurried greeting, had moved towards Margot, around whom he threw his arms, with an energetic clasp, and lifted her from the saddle to the ground. Then he shook hands with her.

"I'm ver mooch glad to see you," said Margot. "Ees your sheep far off?"

"So, they're after you — air they?" said he. "Wal, little one, when they come, you stick to me — mind that; an' I engage to get you off free. Stick to me, though. Be handy, an' I'll take you clar of them."

Claude was now engaged in finding a comfortable place upon which Mimi might recline. The Indian stood as lookout; the deserter busied himself with the horses; the priest stood near, watching Claude and Mimi, while Zac devoted himself to Margot. In the midst of this, the Indian came and said something to the priest. Claude noticed this, and started.

"What is it?" he asked.

"He hears them," said the priest, significantly.

"So soon!" exclaimed Claude. "Then we must scatter. The horses will be of no use. Our last chance is the woods."

In a moment the alarm was made; hasty directions were given for each one to take care of himself, and if he eluded the pursuers, to follow the path to the place where the schooner lay. Meanwhile the horses were to be driven ahead by the Indian as far as possible. The Indian at once went off, together with the deserter, and these two drove the horses before them into the woods, along the path. Then Zac followed. Lifting Margot in his arms, he bore her lightly along, and soon disappeared in the woods.

Then Claude took Mimi in his arms, and hastened as fast as he could towards the shelter of the woods. But Claude had not Zac's strength, and besides, Mimi was more of a dead weight than Margot, so that he could not go nearly so fast. Zac was in the woods, and out of sight, long before Claude had reached the place; and by that time the rest of the party, both horses and men, had all disappeared, with the exception of Père Michel. The good priest kept close by the young man, as though resolved to share his fate, whether in life or death. If it was difficult while carrying Mimi over the path, Claude found it far more so on reaching the woods. Here he dared not keep to the path, for the very object of going to the woods was to elude observation by plunging into its darkest and deepest recesses. Zac had gone there at a headlong rate, like a fox to his covert. Such a speed Claude could not rival, and no sooner did he take one step in the woods, than he perceived the full difficulty of his task. The woods were of the wildest kind, filled with rocks and fallen trees, the surface of the ground being most irregular. At every other step it was necessary to clamber over some obstacle, or crawl under it.

"We cannot hope to go far," said the priest. "Our only course now will be to find some convenient hiding-place. Perhaps they will pass on ahead, and then we can go farther on."

At this very moment the noise of horses and men sounded close behind. One hurried look showed them all. Their pursuers had reached their late halting-place, and were hurrying forward. The place bore traces of their halt, which did not escape the keen eyes of their enemies. At the sight, Claude threw himself down in a hollow behind a tree, with Mimi beside him, while the priest did the same.

The suspicions of the pursuers seemed to have been awakened by the signs which they had seen at the last halting-place. They rode on more slowly. At length they divided, half of them riding rapidly ahead, and the other half moving forward at a walk, and scanning every foot of ground in the open and in the woods.

At last a cry escaped one of them. Claude heard it. The next moment he heard footsteps. The enemy were upon him; their cries rang in his ears. In all the fury of despair, he started to his feet with only one thought, and that was, to sell his life as dearly as possible. But Mimi flung herself in his arms, and the priest held his hands.

"Yield," said the priest. "You can do nothing. There is yet hope."

The next moment Claude was disarmed, and in the hands of his enemies.

CHAPTER XXIV.

ZAC AND MARGOT.

SEIZING Margot in his arms at the first alarm, Zac had fled to the woods. Being stronger than Claude, he was fortunate in having a less unwieldy burden; for Margot did not lie like a heavy weight in his arms, but was able to dispose herself in a way which rendered her more easy to be carried. On reaching the woods, Zac did not at once plunge in among the trees, but continued along the trail for some distance, asking Margot to tell him the moment she saw one of the pursuing party. As Margot's face was turned back, she was in a position to watch. It was Zac's intention to find some better place for flight than the stony and swampy ground at the outer edge of the forest; and as he hurried along, he watched narrowly for a good opportunity to leave the path. At length he reached a place where the ground descended on the other side of the hill, and here he came to some pine trees. There was but little underbrush, the surface of the ground was comparatively smooth, and good progress could be made here without much difficulty. Here, then, Zac turned in. As he hurried onward, he found the pine forest continuing along the whole slope, and but few obstacles in his way. Occasionally a fallen tree lay before him, and this he could easily avoid. Hurrying on, then, under these favorable circumstances, Zac was soon lost in the vast forest, and out of sight as well as out of hearing of all his purposes. Here he might have rested; but still he kept on. He was not one to do things by halves, and chose rather to make assurance doubly sure; and although even Margot begged him to put her down, yet he would not.

"Wal," said he, at last, "'tain't often I have you; an' now I got you, I ain't goin' to let you go for a good bit yet. Besides, you can't ever tell when you're safe. Nothin' like makin' things sure, I say."

With these words Zac kept on his way, though at a slower pace. It was not necessary for him to fly so rapidly, nor was he quite so fresh as when he started. Margot also noticed this, and began to insist so vehemently on getting down, that he was compelled to grant her request. He still held her hand, however, and thus the two went on for some distance farther.

At last they reached a point where there was an abrupt and almost precipitous descent. From this crest of the precipice the eye could wander over a boundless prospect of green forest, terminated in the distance by woodèd hills.

"Wal," said Zac, "I think we may as well rest ourselves here."

"Dat is ver nice," said Margot.

Zac now arranged a seat for her by gathering some moss at the foot of a tree. She seated herself here, and Zac placed himself by her side. He then opened a bag which he carried slung about his shoulders, and brought forth some biscuit and ham, which proved a most grateful repast to his companion.

"Do you tink dey chase us here?" asked Margot.

"Wal, we're safer here, ef they do," said Zac. "We can't be taken by surprise in the rear, for they can't climb up very easy without our seein' 'em; an' as for a front attack, why, I'll keep my eye open: an' I'd like to see the Injin or the Moosoo that can come unawars on me. I don't mind two or three of 'em, any way," continued Zac, "for I've got a couple of bulldogs."

"Boul-dogs?" said Margot, inquiringly.

"Yes, these here," said Zac, opening his frock, and displaying a belt around his waist, which held a brace of pistols. "But I don't expect I'll have to use 'em, except when I heave in sight of the skewner, an' want to hail 'em."

"But we are loss," said Margot, "in dis great woos. How sall we ever get anywhar out of him?"

"O, that's easy enough," said Zac. "I know all about the woods, and can find my way anywhars. My idee is, to go back towards the trail, strike into it, an' move along slowly an' cautiously, till we git nigh the place whar I left the skewner."

Zac waited in this place till towards evening, and then started once more. He began to retrace his steps in a direction which he judged would ultimately strike the trail, along which he had resolved to go. He had weighed the chances, and concluded that this would be his best course. He would have the night to do it in; and if he should come unawares upon any of his enemies, he thought it would be easy to dash into the woods, and escape under the cover of the darkness. Vigilance only was necessary, together with coolness and nerve, and all these qualities he believed himself to have.

. The knowledge of the woods which Zac claimed stood him in good stead on the present occasion; he was able to guide his course in a very satisfactory manner; and about sundown, or a little after, he struck the trail. Here he waited for a short time, watching and listening; and then, having heard nothing whatever that indicated danger, he went boldly forward, with Margot close behind. As they advanced, it grew gradually darker, and at length the night came down. Overhead the moon shone, disclosing a strip of sky where the trees opened above the path. For hours they walked along. No enemy appeared; and at length Zac concluded that they had all dispersed through the woods, at the point where they had first come upon them, and had not followed the path any farther. What had become of Claude he could not imagine, but could only hope for the best.

They rested for about an hour at midnight. Then Zac carried Margot for another hour. After this, Margot insisted on walking. At length, after having thus passed the whole night, the path came to a creek. Here Zac paused.

"Now, little gal," said he, "you may go to sleep till mornin', for I think we've got pooty nigh onto the end of our tramp."

With these words Zac led the way a little distance from the path, and here Margot flung herself upon a grassy knoll, and fell sound asleep, while Zac, at a little distance off, held watch and guard over her.

Several hours passed, and Zac watched patiently. He had not the heart to rouse her, unless compelled by absolute necessity. In this case, however, no necessity arose, and he left her to wake herself.

When at length Margot awoke, the sun was high in the heavens, and Zac only smiled pleasantly when she reproached him for not waking her before.

"O, no harm; no 'casion has riz, an' so you were better havin' your nap. You'll be all the abler to do what you may hev yet before you. An' now, little un, if you're agreed, we'll hev a bite o' breakfast."

A short breakfast, composed of hard biscuit and ham, washed down with cool water from a neighboring brook, served to fortify both for the duties that lay before them; and after this Zac proposed an immediate start.

He led the way along the bank of the creek, and Margot followed. They walked here for about two miles, until at length they came in sight of a small harbor, into which the creek ran. In the distance was the sea; nearer was a headland.

"This here's the place, the i-dentical place," said Zac, in joyous tones. "I knowed it; I was sure of it. Come along, little un. We ain't got much further to go — only to that thar headland; and then, ef I ain't mistook, we'll find the end to our tramp."

With these cheering words he led the way along the shore, until at last they reached the headland. It was rocky and bare of trees. Up this Zac ran, followed by Margot, and soon reached the top.

"All right!" he cried. "See thar!" and he pointed out to the sea.

Margot had already seen it: it was the schooner, lying there at anchor.

"Eet ees de sheep," said Margot, joyously; "but how sall we geet to her?"

"O, they're on the lookout," said Zac. "I'll give signals."

The schooner was not more than a quarter of a mile off. Zac and Margot were on the bare headland, and could easily be seen. On board the schooner figures were moving up and down. Zac looked for a few moments, as if to see whether it was all right, and then gave a peculiar cry, something like the cawing of a crow, which he repeated three times. The sound was evidently heard, for at once there was a movement on board. Zac waved his hat. Then the movement stopped, and a boat shot out from the schooner, with a man in it, who rowed towards the headland. He soon came near enough to be recognized. It was Terry. Zac and Margot hurried to the shore to meet it, and in a short time both were on board the Parson.

Great was the joy that was evinced by Terry at the return of his captain. He had a host of questions to ask about his adventures, and reproached Zac over and over for not allowing him to go also. Jericho showed equal feeling, but in a more emphatic form, since it was evinced in the shape of a substantial meal, which was most welcome to Zac, and to Margot also. As for Biler, he said not a word, but stood with his melancholy face turned towards his master, and his jaws moving as though engaged in devouring something.

"Sure, an' it's glad I am," said Terry, "for it's not comfortable I've been — so it ain't. I don't like bein' shut up here, at all, at all. So we'll just up sail, captain dear, an' be off out of this."

"O, no," said Zac; "we've got to wait for the others."

"Wait — is it?" said Terry.

"Yes."

"Sure, thin, an' there's a sail out beyant. Ye can't see it now, but ye'll see it soon, for it's been batin' up to the land all the mornin'."

"A sail!" exclaimed Zac.

"Yis; an' it's a Frinchman — so it is; an' big enough for a dozen of the likes of us."

Further inquiry elicited the startling information that early in the morning Terry had seen, far away in the horizon, a large ship, which had passed backward and forward while beating up towards the land against a head wind, and was just now concealed behind a promontory on the south. At this Zac felt that his situation was a serious one, and he had to decide what to do. To hoist sail and venture forth to sea would be to discover himself, and lay himself open to certain capture; while to remain where he was gave him the chance of being overlooked. So he decided to remain, and trust to luck. Once, indeed, he thought of going ashore once more, but this thought was at once dismissed. On shore he would be lost. The woods were full of his enemies, and he could hardly hope to reach any English settlement. To himself alone the chance was but slight, while for Margot it was impossible. To leave her now was not to be thought of, and besides, the schooner was the only hope for Claude, who might still be in the neighborhood. The consequence was, that Zac decided to do nothing but remain here and meet his fate, whatever that might be.

Scarcely had he come to this decision, when a sight met his eyes out beyond the southern promontory, where his gaze had been turned. There, moving majestically along the sea, he saw a large frigate. It was not more than a mile away. For about a quarter of an hour the ship sailed along, and Zac was just beginning to hope that he had not been seen, when suddenly she came to, and a boat was lowered.

"She sees us!" said Terry.

Zac made no reply.

Yes; there was no doubt of it. They had been seen. Those on board the ship had been keeping a sharp lookout, and had detected the outline of the schooner sharply defined against the light limestone rock of the headland near which she lay. To escape was not to be thought of. The boat was coming towards them, filled with armed men. Zac stood quite overwhelmed with dejection; and thus he stood as the Parson was boarded and seized by the lieutenant of his French majesty's Vengeur, who took possession of her in the name of his king.

No sooner had Zac found himself in the power of the enemy, than a remarkable change took place in the respective positions of himself and Margot with regard to one another. Thus far he had been her protector; but now she became his. The first words that she spoke to the lieutenant served to conciliate his favor, and secure very respectful treatment for Zac, and seemed to convey such important intelligence that he concluded at once to transfer Margot to the Vengeur, where she could tell her story to the captain.

"Adieu," said she. "We sall soon see again. Do not fear. I make zem let you go."

"Wal, little un, I'll try an' hope. But, mind, unless I get you, I don't much mind what becomes o' me."

Margot, on being taken on board the Vengeur, was at once examined by the captain — the Vicomte de Brissac, who found her statement most important. She contented herself with telling everything that was essential, and did not think it at all necessary for her to state that Zac had already been in the hands of French captors, and had effected an escape. She announced herself as the maid of the Countess Laborde, who had accompanied her father in the ship Arethuse. She narrated the shipwreck, and the rescue by Zac and the young Count de Montresor, the encounter with the Aigle, and the subsequent arrest of Claude. She mentioned the death of Laborde, and the journey to Louisbourg by land, with the escape and pursuit of Claude, the fight with Cazeneau, and his subsequent arrival. She then described their escape, their pursuit and separation, down to the time of speaking. She affirmed that Zac had come here from Minas Basin to save his friend, and was awaiting his arrival when the Vengeur appeared.

The captain listened with the most anxious attention to every word; questioned her most minutely about the reasons why Cazeneau had arrested Claude, and also about his designs on Louisbourg. Margot answered everything most frankly, and was able to tell him the truth, inasmuch as she had enjoyed very much of the confidence of Mimi, and had learned from her about Cazeneau's plans. Captain de Brissac showed no emotion of any kind, whether of sympathy or indignation; but Margot formed a very favorable estimate of his character from his face, and could not help believing that she had won him over as an ally. She could see that her story had produced a most profound impression.

Captain de Brissac was anxious to know what had been the fate of the other fugitives, especially of Claude and Mimi; but of this Margot could, of course, give no information. When she had last seen them they were flying to the woods, and she could only hope that they had been sufficiently fortunate to get under cover before the arrival of the enemy.

Captain de Brissac then sent a crew aboard the Parson, and ordered them to follow the Vengeur to Louisbourg. Upon this new crew Terry looked with careful scrutiny.

"Whisper, captain dear," said he, as he drew up to the meditative Zac. "Here's another lot o' Frinchmen. Is it afther thrying agin that ye are, to give 'em the slip?"

Zac drew a long breath, and looked with a melancholy face at the Vengeur, which was shaking out her sails, and heading east for Louisbourg. On the stern he could see a female figure. He could not recognize the face, but he felt sure that it was Margot.

"Wal," said he, "I guess we'd better wait a while fust, and see how things turn out. The little un's oncommon spry, an' may give us a lift somehow."

CHAPTER XXV.

THE COURT MARTIAL.

CLAUDE was treated roughly, bound, and sent forward on foot; but the representations of Père Michel secured better treatment for Mimi. A litter was made for her, and on this she was carried. As for Père Michel himself, he, too, was conducted back as a prisoner; but the respect of the commander of the soldiers for the venerable priest caused him to leave his hands unbound. After a weary tramp they reached Louisbourg. Cazeneau was at the gate, and greeted them with a sinister smile. Mimi, utterly worn out, both by fatigue and grief, took no notice of him, nor did she hear what he said.

"Take the Countess de Laborde to the Residency."

"Pardon," said the priest; "that lady is now the Countess de Montresor."

At this Cazeneau turned upon him in fury.

"Traitor!" he hissed; "what do you mean?"

"I mean that I married her to the Count de Montresor last night."

"It's a lie! It's a lie!"

"There are witnesses," said Père Michel, "who can prove it."

"It's a lie," said Cazeneau;. "but even if it is true, it won't help her. She'll be a widow before two days.

And as for you, you villain and traitor, you shall bitterly repent your part in last night's work."

Père Michel shrugged his shoulders, and turned away. This act seemed to madden Cazeneau still more.

"Why did you not bind this fellow?" he cried, turning to the commander of the detachment.

"Your excellency, I had his parole."

"A curse on his parole! Take him to the prison with Motier, and bind him like the other."

Upon this, Mimi was taken to the Residency, and Claude and Père Michel were conducted to prison, where both of them were confined. Cazeneau himself then returned to the Residency. The ex-commandant, Florian, was at the door. He saw the whole proceeding, but showed no particular emotion.

Cazeneau regarded him coldly, and Florian returned his gaze with haughty indifference.

"Your plans have not succeeded very well, you see, monsieur," said Cazeneau.

"It is not time enough yet to decide," said Florian.

"To-morrow will decide."

"I think not. You will find, Monsieur le Commandant, that there is public opinion, even in Louisbourg, which cannot be despised."

"Public opinion which favors traitors may safely be despised."

"True," said Florian; and with these words the two parted.

The following day came. A court martial had been called to sit at two in the afternoon. At that hour the session was opened by Cazeneau. The chief officers of the garrison were present. With them came Florian.

"I am sorry, monsieur," said Cazeneau, "that I cannot invite you to a seat in this court."

"By virtue of my military rank," said Florian, "I claim a seat here, if not as judge, at least as spectator. I have come to see that the Count de Montresor has justice."

"There is no such person. We are to try one Motier."

"It can be proved," said Florian, "that he is the Count de Montresor. You yourself arrested him first as such."

"I was mistaken," said Cazeneau.

"As a peer of France, he can appeal to the king; and this court has no final jurisdiction. I call all present to witness this. If my warning is neglected here, it will be felt in a higher quarter. Recollect, monsieur, that I shall soon be able to report to his majesty himself. I flatter myself that my influence at court just now is not inferior to that of the Count de Cazeneau."

"Perhaps, monsieur," said Cazeneau, with a sneer, "you would wish to be commandant a little longer."

"All present," said Florian, "have heard my words. Let them remember that the prisoner is undoubtedly the Count de Montresor, a peer of France. Witnesses can be produced; among others, the Countess de Montresor."

"There is no such person," said Cazeneau, angrily. "That lady is the Countess de Laborde."

"She was married two nights since. All present may take warning by what I have announced. I will say no more."

The words of Florian had made a profound impression. It was no light thing for a colonial court martial to deal with a peer of France. Besides, Florian himself would soon be at court, and could tell his own story. Cazeneau saw that a limit would be placed to his power if he did not manage carefully. He decided to act less harshly, and with more cunning. He therefore assumed a milder tone, assured the court that Florian was mistaken, disclaimed any personal feeling, and finally invited Florian to sit among the judges. Upon this Florian took his seat. The prisoner was now brought forward, and the witnesses prepared.

The charges were then read. These were to the effect that he had been captured while coming to Louisbourg under a suspicious character, calling himself Motier, but pretending to be the son of the outlawed De Montresor; that afterwards he had escaped from confinement, and followed Cazeneau, upon whom he had made a murderous attack.

Claude was then questioned. He told his story fully and frankly as has already been stated. After a severe questioning, he was allowed to sit down, and Père Michel was then summoned.

Père Michel was first asked what he knew about the prisoner. The priest answered, simply,—

"Everything."

"What do you mean? Go on and tell what you know about him."

Père Michel hesitated for a moment, and then, looking at Claude, with a face expressive of the deepest emotion, he said in a low voice,—

"He is my son."

At this declaration amazement filled all present. Claude was affected most of all. He started to his

CLAUDE IN HIS FATHER'S ARMS. Page 249.

feet, and stood gazing at Père Michel with wonder and incredulity.

"I don't understand," said Cazeneau; "at any rate, this shows that he is a low-born adventurer."

At this Père Michel turned to Cazeneau, and said,—

"He is my son, yet neither low-born nor an adventurer. Do you not know — you — who I am? Often have we seen one another face to face within the last few weeks; and yet you have not recognized me! What! have I so changed that not a trace of my former self is visible? Yet what I was once you see now in my son, whom you best know to be what he claims. Yes, gentlemen, I am Eugene, Count de Montresor, and this is my son Claude. — Come, Claude," he continued, "come, my son, to him who has so often yearned to take you to a father's embrace. I hoped to defer this declaration until my name should be freed from dishonor; but in such an hour as this I can keep silent no longer. Yet you know, my son, that the dishonor is not real, and that in the eyes of Heaven your father's name is pure and unsullied."

As he said these words, he moved towards Claude. The young man stood, as pale as death, and trembling from head to foot with excessive agitation. He flung himself, with a low cry, into his father's arms, and leaned his head upon his breast, and wept. The whole court was overcome by this spectacle. There seemed something sacred in this strange meeting of those so near, who for a lifetime had been separated, and had at length been brought together so wonderfully. The silence was oppressive to Cazeneau, who now felt as though all his power was slipping away. It was broken at last by his harsh voice.

"It's false," he said. "The Count de Montresor has been dead for years. It is a piece of acting that may do for the Théâtre Français, but is absurd to sensible men. Gentlemen, these two concocted this whole plan last night when together in their cell. I once knew old Montresor well, and this priest has not a feature in common with him."

The Count de Montresor turned from his son, and faced the court.

"Cazeneau," said he, with scornful emphasis, "now commandant of Louisbourg, once equerry to the Count de Laborde, you never knew me but at a distance, and as your superior. But Florian, here, remembers me, and can testify to my truth. To this court I have only to say that I fled to this country from the result of a plot contrived by this villain; that on the death of my beloved wife I committed my infant son to the care of my faithful valet,— Motier,— and became a missionary priest. For twenty years, nearly, I have labored here among the Acadians and Indians. This year I went to New England in search of Motier. I had already been carrying on correspondence with friends in France, who held out hopes that my wrongs would be righted, and my name saved from dishonor. I did not wish to make myself known to my son till I could give him an unsullied name. I found Motier dead, and learned that my son was going to Louisbourg, *en route* to France. I asked for a passage, and was thus able to be near my son, and study his character. It was I who saved him from prison at Grand Pré; it was I who heard the last words of my former enemy, Laborde; it was I who saved my son, two nights since, from prison. He is guilty of nothing.

If any one is guilty, that one am I alone. I ask, then, that I be considered as a prisoner, and that this innocent young man be set free. But as a peer of France, I claim to be sent to France, where I can be tried by my peers, since this court is one that can have no jurisdiction over one of my rank."

Here the Count de Montresor ceased, and turning to his son, stood conversing with him in a low whisper.

"Every word is true," said Florian. "I assert that Père Michel is the Count de Montresor. I had noticed the likeness formerly; but, as I believed the count to be dead, I thought it only accidental, until a few days ago, when he revealed the truth to me. I recognized him by facts and statements which he made. He has changed greatly since the old days, yet not beyond recognition by a friend. This being the case, then, we have nothing to do, except to send him to France by the next ship. As to the young count, his son, I cannot see that we have any charge against him whatever."

All present, with one exception, had been profoundly moved by the meeting between father and son, nor had they been much less deeply moved by the words of the old count, which, though somewhat incoherent, had been spoken with impressiveness and dignity. The announcement of his lofty rank; the remembrance of his misfortunes, of which most present had heard, and which were universally believed to be unmerited; the assertion that Cazeneau had been the arch villain and plotter, — all combined to increase the common feeling of sympathy for the two before them. This feeling was deepened by Florian's words. His influence, but recently so strong, had not yet passed away.

The new commandant, even under ordinary circumstances, would have been unpopular; but on the present occasion he was detested. The feeling, therefore, was general that nothing ought to be done; and Cazeneau, his heart full of vengeance, found himself well nigh powerless. But he was not a man who could readily give up the purpose of his heart; and therefore he quickly seized the only resource left him.

"Gentlemen," said he, "we must not allow ourselves to be influenced by purely sentimental considerations. I believe that this priest speaks falsely, and that he has imposed upon the sympathies of M. de Florian. Besides, he is an outlaw and a criminal in the eyes of French justice. As to the young man, whom he calls his son, there is the charge of a murderous assault upon me, the commandant of Louisbourg. This must be investigated. But in the present state of mind of those present, I despair of conducting any important trial, and I therefore declare this court adjourned until further notice. Guards, remove these two prisoners, and this time place them in separate cells, where they can no longer have communication with each other."

To this no one raised any objection. As commandant, Cazeneau had the right to adjourn; and, of course, until some actual decision had been reached, he could dispose of them as he saw fit. They could only bring a moral pressure to bear, at least for the present. Father and son were therefore taken back to their prison, and Cazeneau quitted the court, to take counsel with himself as to his future course. He hoped yet to have the game in his own hands. He saw that until Florian was gone it would be difficult, but after that he might manage to control the opinions of the majority of the officers. Florian, however, could not go until the next ship should arrive, and he now awaited its coming with curiosity and eagerness.

He did not have to wait very long.

The court broke up, and the officers talked over the matter among themselves. Florian was now quite communicative, and told them all about the early career of Montresor, and his misfortunes. Cazeneau was the evil cause of all; and Florian was bitter and unsparing in his denunciations of this man's villany. He took care to remind them that Mimi, though the wife of Claude, was still held by him under the pretence that she was his ward, and that Cazeneau, being the creature of the defunct ministry of the late Fleury, could not be kept long in his present office by the hostile ministry which had succeeded. He also assured them that the Montresors had friends among those now in power, and that the old count was anxiously awaiting the arrival of the next ship, in the confident hope that justice would at last be done to him.

By these words, and by this information about things unknown to Cazeneau, Florian deepened the impression which had been made by the events of the trial. All were desirous that the Montresors should at last escape from the machinations of Cazeneau. All looked for the speedy recall and disgrace of Cazeneau himself, and therefore no one was inclined to sacrifice his feelings or convictions for the purpose of gaining favor with one whose stay was to be merely temporary.

While they were yet gathered together discussing these things, they were disturbed by the report of a gun. Another followed, and yet another. All of them hurried to the signal station, from which a view of the harbor was commanded.

There a noble sight appeared before their eyes. With all sail set, a frigate came into the harbor, and then, rounding to, swept grandly up towards the town. Gun after gun sounded, as the salute was given and returned. After her came a schooner.

"It's the Vengeur," said Florian. "I wonder whether Montresor will get his despatches. Gentlemen, I must go aboard."

With these words Florian hurried away from the citadel to the shore.

CHAPTER XXVI.

NEWS FROM HOME.

CAZENEAU had heard the guns, and had learned that the long-expected frigate had arrived, together with a schooner that looked like a prize. To him the matter afforded much gratification, since it offered a quick and easy way of getting rid of Florian, and of making the way easier towards the accomplishment of his own purposes. He did not know that Florian had hurried aboard, nor, had he known, would he have cared. For his own part he remained where he was, awaiting the visit which the captain of the Vengeur would make, to report his arrival. After more than two hours of waiting, it began to strike him that the said captain was somewhat dilatory, and he began to meditate a reprimand for such a neglect of his dignity.

All this time had been spent by Florian on board, where he had much to say to De Brisset, and much to ask of him and also of Margot.

At length a boat came ashore. In the boat were Florian, De Brisset, and Margot. On landing, these three went up to the citadel; and on their way De Brisset was stopped by several of the officers, who were old acquaintances, and were anxious to learn the latest news. Florian also had much to tell them which he had just learned. While they were talking, Margot hurried to the Residency, where she found Mimi, to whom she gave information of a startling kind; so startling, indeed, was it, that it acted like a powerful remedy, and roused Mimi from a deep stupor of inconsolable grief up to life, and hope, and joy, and strength.

The information which De Brisset gave the officers was of the same startling kind, and Florian was able to corroborate it by a despatch which he had received. The despatch was to the effect that he — the Count de Florian — was hereby reinstated in his office as commandant of Louisbourg, and conveyed to him the flattering intelligence that his former administration was favorably regarded by the government, who would reward him with some higher command. With this despatch there came also to Florian, as commandant, a warrant to arrest Cazeneau, the late commandant, on certain charges of fraud, peculation, and malversation in office, under the late ministry. De Brisset also had orders to bring Cazeneau back to France in the Vengeur. These documents were shown to the officers, who were very earnest in their congratulations to Florian.

There were also despatches to the Count de Montresor, the contents of which were known to De Brisset, who also knew that he was now laboring in the colonies as the missionary priest Père Michel. Florian at once took these to the prison where he was confined, acquainted him with the change that had taken place, and set both him and Claude free with his own hands. Then he presented the despatches.

Père Michel, as we may still call him, tore open the

despatch with a trembling hand, and there read that, at last, after so many years, the wrong done him had been remedied, as far as possible; that all his dignities were restored, together with his estates. These last had passed to other hands, but the strong arm of the government was even now being put forth to reclaim them, so that they might be rendered back to the deeply injured man to whom they rightly belonged.

"There, my boy," said Père Michel, as he showed it to his son, "all is right at last; and now you can wear your name and dignity in the face of the world, and not be ashamed."

"O, my father!" said Claude, in a voice which was broken with emotion, "Heaven knows I never was ashamed. I believed your innocence, and wept over your wrongs. I am glad now, not for myself, but for you."

"Where is the Countess de Montresor?" said Père Michel. "She should not be kept in restraint any longer."

Cazeneau all this time sat in his apartment, awaiting the arrival of the captain of the Vengeur and the despatches. The captain at length appeared; but with him were others, the sight of whom awakened strange sensations in his breast. For there was Florian, and with him was Père Michel; Claude was there also, and beyond he saw some soldiers. The sight was to him most appalling, and something in the face and bearing of De Brisset and Florian was more appalling still.

"Monsieur le Comte de Cazeneau," said Florian, "I have the honor to present you with this commission, by which you will see that I am reappointed commandant of Louisbourg. I also have the honor to state that I hold a warrant for your arrest, on certain charges specified therein, and for sending you back to France for trial in the Vengeur, on her return voyage."

Cazeneau listened to this with a pallid face.

"Impossible!" he faltered.

"It's quite true," said De Brisset; "I also have orders to the same effect, which I have already shown to Monsieur le Commandant Florian. There is no possibility of any mistake, or of any resistance. You will therefore do well to submit."

Cazeneau had remained seated in the attitude which he had taken up, when he expected to receive the respectful greeting of his subordinate. The news was so sudden, and so appalling, that he remained motionless. He sat staring, like one suddenly petrified. He turned his eyes from one to another, but in all those faces he saw nothing to reassure him. All were hostile except Père Michel, who alone looked at him without hate. The priest showed the same mild serenity which had always distinguished him. He seemed like one who had overcome the world, who had conquered worldly ambition and worldly passion, and had passed beyond the reach of revenge.

Cazeneau saw this. He rose from his seat, and fell at the feet of Père Michel.

"Pardon," he faltered; "Comte de Montresor, do not pursue a fallen man with your vengeance."

At this unexpected exhibition, all present looked with scorn. They had known Cazeneau to be cruel and unscrupulous; they had not suspected that he was cowardly as well. Père Michel also preserved an unchanged demeanor.

"You are mistaken, Cazeneau," he said. "I feel no desire for vengeance. I seek none. Moreover, I have no influence or authority. You must direct your prayers elsewhere."

Upon this the wretched man turned to Florian.

"Come, come," said Florian, impatiently. "This will never do. Rise, monsieur. Remember that you are a Frenchman. Bear up like a man. For my part, I can do nothing for you, and have to obey orders."

Cazeneau's break down was utter, and effectually destroyed all sympathy. His present weakness was compared with his late vindictiveness, and he who had just refused mercy to others could hardly gain pity on himself. He only succeeded in utterly disgracing himself, without inspiring a particle of commiseration. Still Florian was not cruel, and contented himself with keeping his prisoner in a room in the Residency, satisfied that there was no possibility of escape. Some of the officers, however, were loud in their condemnation of Florian's mildness, and asserted that the dungeon and the chains, which had been inflicted by him on the Montresors, should be his doom also. But Florian thought otherwise, and held him thus a prisoner until the Vengeur returned. Then Cazeneau was sent back to be tried and convicted. His life was spared; but he was cast down to hopeless degradation and want, in which state his existence ultimately terminated.

Before the scene with Cazeneau was over, Claude had gone away and found his wife. Already Mimi's strength had begun to return, and her new-born hope, and the rush of her great happiness, coming, as it did, after so much misery and despair, served to restore her rapidly.

"I should have died if this had lasted one day more," said she.

"But now it is all over, Mimi, dearest," said Claude, "and you must live for me. This moment repays me for all my sufferings."

"And for mine," sighed Mimi.

Margot saw that her mistress had for the present an attendant who was more serviceable than herself, and now all her thoughts turned to that faithful friend whom she had been compelled for the time to leave, but whom she had not for one moment forgotten. She waited patiently till she could get a chance to speak to Claude, and then told him what he did not know yet — that Zac was still a prisoner. At that intelligence, his own happiness did not allow him to delay to serve his friend. He at once hurried forth to see De Brisset. To him he explained Zac's position in such forcible language, that De Brisset at once issued an order for the release of himself and his schooner, without any conditions, and the recall of his seamen. To make the act more complete, the order was committed to Margot, who was sent in the ship's boat to the schooner.

On the arrival of this boat, Zac seemed quite indifferent to the safety of the schooner, and only aware of the presence of Margot. He held her hand, and stood looking at her with moistened eyes, until after the seamen of the Vengeur had gone. Terry looked away; Jericho vanished below, with vague plans about a great supper. Biler gazed upon Louisbourg with a pensive eye and a half-eaten turnip.

"I knowed you'd be back, little un," said Zac; "I felt it; an', now you've come, don't go away agin."

"O, but I haf to go to ze comtesse," said Margot; "zat ees — to-day — "

"Go back to the countess! Why, you ain't goin' to give me up — air you?" said Zac, dolefully.

"O, no, not eef you don't want me to," said Margot. "But to-day I moos go to ze comtesse, an' afterward you sall ask her, eef you want me."

At this, which was spoken in a timid, hesitating way, Zac took her in his arms, and gave her a tremendous smack, which Terry tried hard not to hear.

"Wal," said he, "thar's Père Michel, that's a Moosoo an' a Roman Catholic; but he'll do."

"O, but you moos not talk of Père Michel till you see ze comtesse," said Margot; "an' now I sall tank you to take me back to her, or send me back by one of de men."

Zac did not send her back, but took her back to the shore himself. Then the fortifications of Louisbourg — the dread and bugbear of all New England — closed him in; but Zac noticed nothing of these. It was only Margot whom he saw; and he took her to the citadel, to the Residency. On his arrival, Claude came forth to greet him, with beaming eyes and open arms. Père Michel greeted him, also, with affectionate cordiality. For the simple Yankee had won the priest's heart, as well on account of his own virtues as for his son's sake. He also took enough interest in him to note his dealings with Margot, and to suggest to him, in a sly way, that, under the circumstances, although Zac was a bigoted Protestant, a Roman Catholic priest could do just as well as a Protestant parson. Whereupon Zac went off with a broad grin, that lasted for weeks.

The postponement of Florian's departure caused

some disappointment to that worthy gentleman, which, however, was alleviated by the thought that he had been able to benefit his injured friend, and bring a villain to punishment; and also by the thought that his departure to France would not be long delayed. To those friends he devoted himself, and sought by every means in his power to make their recollections of Louisbourg more pleasant than they had thus far been. Claude, and his bride, and his father were honored guests at the Residency, where they were urged to remain as long as they could content themselves, and until they could decide about their future movements.

For now, though the name of Montresor had been redeemed, and justice had at last been done, it was not easy for them to decide about their future movements. Père Michel, after some thought, had at length made up his mind, and had given Claude the benefit of his opinion and his advice.

"I have made up my mind," said he. "I will never go back to France. What can I do in France? As a French noble, I should be powerless; as a priest, useless. France is corrupt to the heart's core. The government is corrupt. The whole head is sick, the whole heart faint. Ministry succeeds to ministry, not by means of ability, not from patriotism or a public spirit, but simply through corrupt favoritism. There are no statesmen in France. They are all courtiers. In that court every man is ready to sell himself for money. There is no sense of honor. At the head of all is the worst of all, the king himself, who sets an example of sin and iniquity, which is followed by all the nation. The peasantry are slaves, trodden in the dust, without hope and without spirit. The nobles are obsequious time-servers and place-hunters. The old sentiment of chivalry is dead. I will never go to such a country. Here, in this land, where I have lived the best part of my life, I intend to remain, to labor among these simple Acadians, and these children of the forest, and to die among them.

"As for you, my son, France is no place for you. The proper place for you, if you wish to lead a virtuous and honorable life, is among the people who look upon you as one of themselves, with whom you have been brought up. Your religion, my son, is different from mine; but we worship the same God, believe in the same Bible, put our trust in the same Saviour, and hope for the same heaven. What can France give you that can be equal to what you have in New England? She can give you simply honors, but with these the deadly poison of her own corruption, and a future full of awful peril. But in New England you have a virgin country. There all men are free. There you have no nobility. There are no down-trodden peasants, but free farmers. Every man has his own rights, and knows how to maintain them. You have been brought up to be the free citizen of a free country. Enough. Why wish to be a noble in a nation of slaves? Take your name of Montresor, if you wish. It is yours now, and free from stain. Remember, also, if you wish, the glory of your ancestors, and let that memory inspire you to noble actions. But remain in New England, and cast in your lot with the citizens of your own free, adopted land."

Such were the words of the priest, and Claude's training had been such that they chimed in altogether with his own tastes. He did not feel himself entirely capable of playing the part of a noble in such a country as that France which his father described; of associating with such a society, or of courting the favor of such a king. Besides, his religion was the religion of his mother; and her fate was a sufficient warning. And so it was that Claude resolved to give up all thoughts of France, and return to the humble New England farm. If from the wreck of the Montresor fortunes anything should be restored, he felt that he could employ it better in his own home than in the home of his fathers; while the estate of Laborde, which Mimi would inherit, would double his own means, and give him new resources.

This, then, was his final decision; and, though it caused much surprise to Florian, he did not attempt to oppose it. Mimi raised no objection. She had no ties in France; and wherever her husband might be was welcome to her. And so Zac was informed that Claude would hire his schooner once more, to convey himself and his wife back to Boston, together with his father, who, at their urgent solicitation, consented to pay them a visit.

But Zac had purposes of his own, which had to be accomplished before setting forth on his return. He wished to secure the services of Père Michel, which services were readily offered; and Zac and Margot were made one in the very chapel which had witnessed the marriage of Claude and Mimi.